Dummies Guide to Starting Your Own Business

Your Definitive Guide to Launching a Successful Business Quickly and Efficiently—Gain an Edge

Wealthwise Publications

© Copyright 2024 - All rights reserved.

The content contained within this book may not be reproduced, duplicated or transmitted without direct written permission from the author or the publisher.

Under no circumstances will any blame or legal responsibility be held against the publisher, or author, for any damages, reparation, or monetary loss due to the information contained within this book, either directly or indirectly.

Legal Notice:

This book is copyright protected. It is only for personal use. You cannot amend, distribute, sell, use, quote or paraphrase any part, or the content within this book, without the consent of the author or publisher.

Disclaimer Notice:

Please note the information contained within this document is for educational and entertainment purposes only. All effort has been executed to present accurate, up to date, reliable, complete information. No warranties of any kind are declared or implied. Readers acknowledge that the author is not engaged in the rendering of legal, financial, medical or professional advice. The content within this book has been derived from various sources. Please consult a licensed professional before attempting any techniques outlined in this book.

By reading this document, the reader agrees that under no circumstances is the author responsible for any losses, direct or indirect, that are incurred as a result of the use of the information contained within this document, including, but not limited to, errors, omissions, or inaccuracies.

Table of Contents

INTRODUCTION 1

CHAPTER 1: FROM CONCEPT TO BUSINESS 5
    GETTING READY 6
    FINDING YOUR BUSINESS IDEA 7
    MARKET RESEARCH MADE SIMPLE 9
    ADVANCED TIPS 11

CHAPTER 2: BUSINESS PLANNING 13
    COMPONENTS OF A BUSINESS PLAN 14
    BUSINESS STRUCTURES 16
    LEGAL AND REGULATORY FACTORS 18
    ADVANCED TIPS 20

CHAPTER 3: FUNDING 23
    Angel Investors 23
    Bootstrapping 24
    Crowdfunding 24
    Friends and Family 25
    Grants and Government Programs 26
    Personal Savings and Assets 26
    Small Business Loans 26
    BASIC FINANCIAL MANAGEMENT SKILLS 27
    ADVANCED TIPS 29

CHAPTER 4: BUILDING YOUR BRAND 33
    CREATING A BRAND IDENTITY 34
    BUILDING BRAND AWARENESS 36
    MARKETING ON A BUDGET 37
    SALES STRATEGIES FOR BEGINNERS 39
    ADVANCED TIPS 40

CHAPTER 5: FINANCIAL MANAGEMENT 43
    ESTABLISH FINANCIAL GOALS AND BUDGET 44
    CASH FLOW MANAGEMENT 45
    DEBT MANAGEMENT 47

CHAPTER 6: OVERCOME COMMON STARTUP CHALLENGES ... 51

- Competition ... 52
- Barriers to Market Entry ... 53
- Build a Strong Team ... 54
- Stress and Burnout ... 55
- Dynamic Market ... 56
- Advanced Tips ... 56

CHAPTER 7: GROWTH AND SCALING ... 59

- Growth Objectives ... 59
  - *What are Your KPIs?* ... *60*
- Optimize Business Processes ... 61
- Expand Products or Service Offerings ... 62
- Explore Strategic Partnerships ... 63
- Advanced Tips ... 64

CHAPTER 8: THE ROAD TO RECURRING INCOME ... 67

- Outsourcing ... 69
- Hiring the Right People ... 70
- Running a Simple, Efficient Operation ... 71

CHAPTER 9: PASSION AND MOTIVATION ... 73

- Maintain the Passion, Against All Odds ... 74
- Be Inspired ... 77
  - *Oprah Winfrey* ... *78*
  - *Melanie Perkins—Canva* ... *78*
  - *Elon Musk* ... *79*
  - *Confucius* ... *79*

CHAPTER 10: LOOK TO THE FUTURE ... 81

- Handling Challenges and Setbacks ... 82
- Growing Your Team ... 85
- The Future of Your Business ... 86

BONUS CHAPTER: 30-DAY BUSINESS LAUNCH CHECKLIST ... 89

- Day 1-5: Lay the Foundation ... 89
- Day 6-10: Branding and Your Online Presence ... 90
- Day 11-15: Marketing & Sales Strategy ... 92
- Day 16-21: Operational Setup ... 93
- Day 22-25: Post-Launch Activities ... 94
- Day 26 and Beyond: Post-Launch Activities ... 95

CONCLUSION ... 97

GLOSSARY ... 99

REFERENCES ... 103

Introduction

Setting up a business is one of the most rewarding things you can do today, yet it could also be a daunting task if you don't know how to approach the nitty-gritties of entrepreneurship. One of the first realities that hits you as an entrepreneur is that this venture will be filled with uncertainties, and challenges along the way. However, that's not supposed to hold you back. If anything, conquering the challenges along the way makes you bolder, builds your confidence, and strengthens your resilience. Every step from ideation to research, funding, marketing, and ultimately growing the business is an opportunity to learn and get better.

Without proper guidance you can easily get overwhelmed, miss some important details or make mistakes that could derail your business prospects. That's where this book comes in, giving you insight into starting and managing your business the right way. We won't just talk about setting up your business; we'll dive deeper into actionable steps, breaking down the complexities and giving you a clear blueprint to bring your vision to life.

The beauty of business is that it's everyone's playground. Therefore, whether you're a student trying to find your way into entrepreneurship, a small business owner who's already running a business, or a professional who wishes to transition into entrepreneurship to diversify your investment portfolio, this book is for you. Together, we shall explore a wide range of essential topics in setting up and running a business.

Some of the lessons you will take from this book include:

- Formulating business ideas, and validating them to ensure you provide tangible solutions to immediate customer needs.

- Creating a solid business plan that will not only become the roadmap of your business venture, but can also come in handy when you need financial support.

- Accounting and financial management: useful skills to help you know how your money works in the business, and more importantly, how to run a sound and financially healthy operation

- Building a resilient business that will not only withstand economic pressure, but also become a successful source of recurring income.

- Different sources of funding, bearing in mind that you might not have the finances to fully start and support the venture as outlined in your business plan.

- A growth plan to help you scale up operations, expand your reach, while keeping a lean operation with an emphasis on long-term growth.

We will sum it all up with an elaborate 30-day business launch checklist, that essentially gives you practical tips on what to do within the first month of launching your business.

Every chapter in this book is structured in a manner that explores both foundational concepts and advanced tips, making it easier to use the book as both a beginner guide, and as reference material for seasoned entrepreneurs. Where applicable, we will also include some real-life examples to give you first-hand experience of theory-to-practice as you progress on your entrepreneurial journey.

I do encourage you to not only read this book with an open mind, but to be proactive while at it. Adaptability, persistence, and courage are key traits you must embrace in your entrepreneurship journey. With the right mindset, this guide will help you navigate different challenges and explore various opportunities that come your way.

Remember, there's more to business success than just having the resources to back a brilliant business idea. Entrepreneurship is a journey of learning and growth, so you must cultivate a mindset that challenges you to pursue greatness, seek continuous development, and stay focussed on your goals.

I'm thrilled to be a part of your journey into entrepreneurship, and hope this is the beginning of something great—a transformative force in your life that will push you to the greatest heights in your pursuits.

Chapter 1:

From Concept to Business

Owning a thriving business is a brilliant idea, a dream for many people. If there's one thing a lot of people learned from the COVID-19 pandemic, it's that you cannot survive on a single source of income. Since then, there's been a surge in the number of people exploring options to diversify their sources of income, with many looking to set up businesses. While the pandemic might have been a fitting catalyst, the need to diversify your income has been a fact since the concept of income became part of the human experience. Any economist or financial advisor you engage with about your personal finances will always advise you to consider looking for additional sources of income, at least to ease the burden on your primary paycheck.

There are lots of business ideas that you can explore. A common mistake that many first-time business owners make is to try and replicate what someone else is doing. This rarely works out because, even though you might like someone else's business idea, you do not know what drives them to pursue that idea. More importantly, you do not understand the nature of their market demographics and how those plays into their overall business structure. With that in mind, I'd advise you to start by figuring out what works for you, how the business you're considering fits not only into your immediate financial plans, but more importantly, whether it aligns with your overall goals for the future.

In this chapter, we will explore the first, and most important step in setting up a business: finding an ideal business idea. This always seems like a simple concept, yet it's where many people lose the plot. As you read through this chapter, you'll be able to answer the following crucial questions:

- What steps do I need to take to start my own business?

- How do I come up with a business idea?

- How do I conduct market research to validate my business idea?

Getting Ready

You're setting up an exciting, and hopefully, rewarding experience. How do you begin? How do you know you are ready? There are as many ways to approach a business as there are opportunities. For each opportunity, there will always be different dynamics to explore. To improve your chances of success, take the guesswork out of the equation. Your money is at stake here, so the last thing you want to do is build a business on the foundation of ifs and maybes.

Start by getting in the right mindset. We see successful businesses all the time, read about their grass-to-grace tales, but never truly get the picture of the effort they put into the foundation. How did they get the dream on paper? How did they start building the business? How did they make their first pitch? I'll reiterate at this point that this is your journey, so do not make the mistake of comparing it to someone else's. You can learn from what they have done, but never try to copy and paste what they are doing.

What do you really want to do? Where do you see yourself in the next five or ten years? What problems are you trying to solve in the community? What personal problems would you wish to solve through your business? If you don't already have a business idea, the following questions could set you on the right path:

- What are you good at?

- What could be done to make something you've been struggling with feel easier?

- What do people often come to you for advice about?

- If you had the resources, what's the one thing you've always wanted to do?

- You find yourself before a Shark Tank panel and have 5-10 minutes to pitch an idea—what do you talk about?

Some of these questions might seem crazy, but rest assured that nothing is impossible. Brilliant ideas often come from things or concepts that we never imagined possible in the first place. The questions above could lead you to an amazing idea for your first business. If you already have a business running, you might find an answer that helps you upscale. Whichever idea you choose, find out whether someone's already doing it, and whether it's profitable or not. If it's a profitable idea, explore expansion dynamics, so that from the very beginning, you know you're setting up something with endless possibilities. The last thing you want to do is to put your time, effort, and resources into a dead-end concept.

Finding Your Business Idea

From the questions you explored in the previous section, you probably have a number of ideas already. However, like most entrepreneurs, these ideas circling your head could lead to another problem—which is the most ideal of them all? There are lots of factors that could influence your decision-making process, all which have a profound impact on the direction you take with the business. At the end of the day, an ideal business model should be fitting in terms of scalability, profitability, your budget, and whether you can devote ample time to it.

First, let's brainstorm different ideas. List the random business ideas you've thought about, whether from answering the questions above or otherwise. An ideal idea should be compatible with your personal objectives because this is where you draw the motivation when things get rough. It could also be a hobby, but most importantly, it should be something that is within your abilities. Motivation and the right mindset are crucial because the journey into entrepreneurship isn't always an easy one. You must keep going, especially when the odds are stacked against you. After brainstorming ideas, research to find out more about the businesses you are interested in. understand how they work, what they require, the market dynamics, target audience, and so on. This gives you a good picture of what lies ahead. At the end of the research stage, you'll probably have crossed out some ideas because their dynamics don't align with your resources. Remember, your business idea doesn't necessarily have to be the next Apple, but if that works for you then go for it.

Here are some useful questions that can help you shed more light on the cost of running your ideal business idea:

- How are you funding the business?

- How much time can you commit to the business?

- Do you need to set up a physical business or can you run it online?

- How does this business align with your passions or hobbies?

- Are you selling a product or service?

- What personal skills do you possess that could be valuable in this business?

- How fast can you scale the business?

- Other than financial support, what kind of help do you require?

- Are you running it alone, or with a partner?

Overheads are an important factor to consider at this point. A common mistake many beginners make is to focus on how much they can make from the business, without thinking about the overheads. The cost of running a business eats into your profits, so this is one factor you should never underestimate. Whatever business idea you choose, its nature is, in fact, the most important part of your journey. The nature of the business determines a lot of things, from financing to marketing, investment prospects, and the target market.

Market Research Made Simple

Market research helps you figure out the viability of your business. Up to this point, you've been looking at how the business idea works for you. You've explored your goals, objectives, whether you have the funds for it, the time, and so on. All these factors point to you. With market research, you're trying to establish whether your potential customers will be receptive to the business idea. After all, you need customers to take this idea to the next level.

In this stage, you'll explore industry trends, the target audience, market dynamics, and any other factor that could influence the customer-facing side of the business. You will also assess the strengths and weaknesses of your business idea and weigh them against the competition. If other businesses are already in the market, the goal is to establish how they are coping within the current market conditions. You can learn a thing or two from their approach, which will go a long way toward setting you on the right path.

Ultimately, market research is about testing your ideas, mostly against factors that you have no direct influence over. Here's a brief guide to help you evaluate your business idea:

- Have clear objectives on what you want to learn about the business through market research. For example, potential demand, customer needs, or a thorough competitor assessment.

- Identify the target market for your business. Who are they? What is their gender? What's their income level? What are their social interests? The more you know about your target market, the easier it is to develop products or services that address their immediate needs.

- Choose an ideal data collection method depending on the nature of your business. You can use Google Forms, or tools like SurveyMonkey to obtain quantitative data from your target audience.

- Beyond interviews, go a step further and review industry reports, data available in public records, or competitor social media platforms, websites, reviews, or available financial reports to get more information on the market dynamics.

- Analyze data obtained from your research process to identify correlations, trends, or patterns. In this process, you're trying to establish distinct themes, customer sentiments, and even draw insight from the data, which sheds more light on the nature of the market.

- Based on the assessment above, you now have enough information to establish whether the market has sufficient demand for your business idea. How well can you address the needs or pain points of your customers? Do you feel customers will be willing to pay for the products or services at the price you intend to offer?

- As you assess the market size, explore possible growth opportunities in this sector. If you were to diversify your business into a different direction, for example, do you think your customers would be willing to roll along with you?

- Finally, use the insight and feedback obtained from the research process to refine and improve your business idea. Are you going to proceed with the business as it is, or will you shake things up a bit? Test the business idea to establish its resilience in different market conditions.

Let's explore a hypothetical scenario where you're setting up a sustainable clothing line. First, your business objective is to establish demand among millennials—at this point, you already know this product will be a hit with millennials, probably aged 25-40, who live in urban and upmarket neighborhoods.

Notable competitors in this sector include:

- Patagonia

- Everlane

- Girlfriend Collective
- Kotn
- Pact
- Able

For data collection, conduct surveys on social media, engage fashion-conscious millennials and influencers, conduct video interviews, and monitor shopping behavior, particularly in eco-friendly stores.

From your survey responses, you'll learn about customer preferences, desired price point, clothing themes, customer willingness to pay at certain prices, and other information to help you evaluate competitor strategies.

Use the feedback above to adjust your business idea. For example, if you intend to primarily deal in formal wear, you could switch to casual wear or incorporate it into your business model if that's what your audience needs.

Advanced Tips

The discussion above centers around an initial concept approach for first-time business owners. If you have some experience in the business world already, or perhaps you're looking to expand into a different territory, here are some advanced tips that could help you pivot your idea from concept to a functional business:

- Since you have an idea of your potential customers, engage them to understand their pain points. You can use interviews, surveys, or social media listening to identify gaps in the business process that you could exploit and create a business that addresses their immediate needs.

- Think about the kind of challenges you experience at work. Solutions to your personal frustrations could actually lead you to some innovative business ideas.

- Review industry trends and reports to identify recurring inefficiencies and challenges, whose solutions could reveal ideal opportunities.

- Explore emerging technologies in an industry you're interested in, for example: the Internet of Things (IoT), Artificial Intelligence (AI), or blockchain technology. How can you leverage such technologies to solve existing problems?

- Consider a spin-off of a brilliant concept. For example, if you work for a big company, review some of their successful innovations or projects and consider how you can create a standalone business from that. We've seen this concept in the entertainment industry, where a successful TV series brings forth one or a few spin-off shows that explore different dynamics that the original show might have overlooked, or ideas that the fans felt could have been explored further. For example, *Young Sheldon* was a successful spin-off from the success of *The Big Bang Theory*.

Whether you're working on your first ever business idea or exploring advanced tips, the most important lesson in this section is that you must be ready to innovate. As an entrepreneur, innovation sets you apart from the competition. Think outside the box. Whatever business idea you come up with, make sure it's something that you can refine, upgrade, or upscale to not only align with the needs of your customers, but more importantly, to fit into your overall financial framework.

Chapter 2:

Business Planning

In the previous chapter, we explored how to identify business ideas and assess their viability through market research. Now that you've figured out what you want to do, the next step is drawing up a plan which will become the blueprint for your success. As you read through this chapter, you'll be able to answer the following questions:

- How do I create a business plan?

- What are the components of a business plan?

- What business structure should I choose?

- What legal requirements and regulations do I need to consider when starting a business?

A business plan is one of the most important documents for your business. It outlines your plan of action—how you get from setting up the business to achieving your goals. In this manner, the plan creates a sense of clarity for your investors, acting as proof of the viability of your business. While you'll need a business plan when starting the business, you can also create separate business plans for various projects through the course of your business.

Ideally, a business plan serves the following functions:

- Helps you predict and create a risk management plan.

- Acts as a yardstick for progress, helping you assess business growth over time.

- Outlines clear steps for diversifying into new markets.

- Sets clear timelines for pursuing and achieving business goals.

Components of a Business Plan

The structure and components of your business plan will depend on the nature of your business, and the purpose of the plan. Generally, since the plan outlines your goals for the business, it should have the following components:

- **Executive Summary**

This is a general overview of your entire business plan, highlighting the contents at a glance. This summary should also include your mission statement, and the products or services you intend to offer. Since you're just setting up the business, include your reasons for starting the business.

- **Business Description**

Provide an accurate description of your business, with an emphasis on your goals, target customers, industry overview, competitors, and major trends that influence investor or customer activity in that sector. Include your experience in the field, or if you have a team, include their combined experience and how it gives you a competitive edge in the market.

- **Market Analysis**

This section explains crucial details about your target audience, for example: who are they? Where are they? What are their pain points? What are their needs, and how do you intend to meet them? Where do they spend their time? (if this is relevant). Provide as much information about the customer demographics as possible, so that it's clear how your business intends to appeal to this audience.

- **Marketing or Sales Plan**

This section builds on the market analysis information, showing how you will get your products or services to the customers. You should include your marketing or promotion strategies, prospective pricing strategy, possible reasons why customers would buy from you instead of the competition, and your unique selling proposal (USP).

- **Management and Organization**

This section outlines your leadership structure. Who is in charge? If you're working with a team, what's your organization structure? List all the leaders in your business, their qualifications, roles, and responsibilities.

- **Products and Services Description**

Give an apt description of your products or services, including all the necessary information, for example, a manufacturing plan, their longevity, customer needs they will meet, and the cost of production.

- **Competitive Analysis**

Explain how your business stands up to the competition. This includes a SWOT analysis of your competitors, and how your business will exploit their weaknesses to gain a footing in the market. Include the qualities that make your business stand out from the competition, and any possible challenges that you might experience when getting into the market.

- **Operating Plan**

This section outlines your logistical approach, and will include the business location, intellectual property, patents, copyrights, and a breakdown of the number of employees you'll need in each department.

- **Financial Projection**

This section will cover your revenue plan. Do you have the money needed to start and run the business? If not, where will you source it? Include financial statement projections, especially the statement of expected cash flows.

- **Appendices**

In this section, include any additional information that could support your business plan, for example, licenses and permits, any relevant legal documentation, product pictures, marketing materials, and documents outlining your marketing research.

Business Structures

How do you intend to run the business? This decision could influence other aspects of your business, for example, your insurance contract, financing, and tax obligation. The ideal business structure depends on the nature of your business, and at times, your personal preference. Here are some of your options:

- **Sole Proprietorships**

This is the simplest business structure, ideal for most small business owners and startups. All you need is to register and obtain relevant licenses according to your local government. You have complete control over all decisions and are personally liable for all debts and obligations. Sole proprietorships have direct tax benefits because you report business income on your personal tax return.

- **LLC (Limited Liability Company)**

This is a flexible business structure that combines the limited liability protection of a corporation with the tax benefits and simplicity of a partnership. Owners, known as members, are protected from personal liability for business debts and claims. LLCs can choose to be taxed as a sole proprietorship, partnership, or corporation, offering versatility in management and tax planning.

- **General Partnership**

A general partnership involves two or more individuals who share ownership and management responsibilities equally or according to an agreement. Each partner is personally liable for the debts and obligations of the business, making them jointly and severally responsible. Profits and losses are passed through to the partners' personal tax returns, avoiding corporate taxation.

- **Limited Partnership**

A limited partnership consists of at least one general partner and one or more limited partners. The general partner manages the business and assumes personal liability, while limited partners contribute capital and share profits but have limited liability and no management authority. Limited partnerships are commonly used for raising capital while maintaining control within a small group of general partners.

- **C Corporation**

A C corporation is a legal entity separate from its owners, providing limited liability protection to the shareholders. It can raise capital by issuing stock and is subject to corporate taxation, meaning profits are taxed at the corporate level and again as dividends on shareholders' personal tax returns. C Corporations offer perpetual existence and are ideal if you're planning to diversify your business into other sectors, or if you want to go public.

- **S Corporation**

An S corporation is similar to a C corporation in terms of limited liability and corporate formalities but offers different tax treatment. It allows profits and losses to be passed through to shareholders' personal tax returns, avoiding double taxation. S corporations are limited to 100 shareholders and must meet specific IRS criteria, making them suitable for small to mid-sized businesses looking for tax advantages.

Legal and Regulatory Factors

It takes a lot of creativity to start and run a successful business. Unfortunately, many entrepreneurs get caught up in the creative freedom, so much that they don't realize when their seemingly innocent actions contravene legal and regulatory requirements in the industries within which they operate. As a rule of thumb, it's always advisable to engage an attorney to help you navigate the legal framework around your business. However, even without an attorney, there are some requirements that every business owner should know about. Let's explore some of them here:

- **Registered Business Name**

You should operate under a registered business name. Once you choose the ideal business structure as outlined in the previous section, research and choose a business name that has not been legally claimed. While you can be as creative as you want with business names, make sure it's something your customers can easily recognize. Registration is important because it gives your brand legal protections against copyright infringement.

- **Taxation**

Consult a tax attorney to help you understand your tax obligations, and the necessary tax identification numbers you need to operate in your jurisdiction. You'll need this information to open a business bank account, and to apply for permits and licenses. Your tax information will also be required when hiring employees.

- **Permits and Licenses**

Permits and licenses vary by state, so consult your local tax attorney. Requirements depend on your business activity, industry, location, and government rules. Each jurisdiction has unique regulations you must follow.

- Partnership Agreement

If you're ever bringing someone on to help you manage the business in any capacity, make sure you draft a partnership agreement that outlines their rights and responsibilities even if they are not coming on as an official partner. This is a crucial step that can help you resolve disputes amicably.

- Copyrights, Patents, and Trademarks

Protect your brand from the get-go by applying for copyrights, patents, and trademarks. This is particularly important if your product or service involves intellectual property that could be copied, especially if you're in the creative industry. Note that someone could easily beat you to copyrighting your work, denying you revenue from the proceeds of your creative work, and more importantly, barring you from using your own work because they legally own it.

- Type of Employees

As your business grows, you might need to hire employees in various capacities. Before you bring anyone on, make sure you clearly state the nature of their role. This is important because employee classifications usually influence your tax obligations, the benefits the employees are entitled to, their wages, and other aspects of their employment. Your job posting should state clearly whether you're hiring interns, seasonal employees, independent contractors, temporary employees, part-time, or full-time employees.

Consider the pros and cons, for example, of hiring an employee versus a contractor. With a contractor, you don't have to incur costs like health insurance and retirement plans, reducing your overall costs. Contractors also offer flexibility and can be hired for specific projects, which can be a bonus for your short-term needs.

Hiring employees instead of contractors gives you more control over your work processes and schedules, which are ideal for the long-term stability of your business, and to maintain company culture. Over time, some employees become more invested in your success, and might even be more willing to go the extra mile for you than a contractor would. Once you understand these differences, you can then select an employee type that fits into your overall business model.

- **Insurance**

Speak to your insurer about protecting your business. This isn't necessarily a legal requirement, but a risk mitigation strategy to protect your business from costly damages like fire, theft, or even lawsuits. You could get general liability insurance to protect yourself against claims like damage to people's property, personal injury or bodily injury.

Workers' compensation insurance protects you when your employees are injured in the line of duty, and pays for funeral costs, medical care, death benefits, and income compensation as they recover, so you don't have to dig into your pockets for compensation.

Commercial property insurance covers the cost of damage to buildings or machines used in your operations, with notable exceptions for natural disasters like floods and earthquakes. If you operate in areas prone to such events, some insurance companies offer special protections for such.

Note that legal requirements will depend on your jurisdiction, so even though the points above might apply across the board, the finer details might not. This is where your tax attorney comes in handy.

Advanced Tips

Further to the points we discussed above, here are some advanced tips to help your business planning process:

- Go the extra mile in competitor benchmarking, beyond the SWOT analysis when assessing the competition. Create elaborate maps of the customer journey to understand their pain points and touchpoints, which could reveal ideal opportunities for engagement.

- To create a product or service that stands out from the competition, clearly define your unique selling point (USP) in the business plan. Go further and analyze the value chain to identify areas where you can improve efficiency or create additional value to your customers.

- Outline your customer value proposition (CVP), clearly stating specific benefits that your product or service will provide to different types of customers. This way, you're creating customer niches within your business instead of serving a generalized market. This could also help you create different price points for your customers.

- Provide more details for your financial projections, including most likely scenarios, worst case, and best case scenarios. This information gives you a clearer picture of your business prospects in different market conditions.

- Establish the ideal break-even point for your business to determine the minimum possible sales you need to make to cover the cost of operation. Include a detailed monthly cash flow projection assessment to help you manage liquidity, and ensure you can meet the financial obligations of your day-to-day operations.

- Create an elaborate risk management plan, which includes identifying possible risks, assessing their impact, and developing appropriate mitigation strategies. The goal here is to have an astute contingency plan for crucial risks beyond your control, for example, a market downturn, changes to the regulatory framework, or supply chain disruptions.

In the long run, proper business planning should be flexible, robust, and dynamic in a manner that not only sets a clear path for your business, but also becomes the blueprint on which you can run a lean business, helping you adapt to different challenges, and exploit opportunities as they arise.

Chapter 3:

Funding

Your business plan is ready. This is where the hard work begins. Funding has always been a challenge for many aspiring entrepreneurs. In fact, there are many who managed to get their business ideas off the ground, but due to insufficient funding, they simply could not keep the operation going. In this section, we will address one of the most important questions every business owner ponders—where can I get funding for my startup?

When you're setting up or growing a business, most people limit their thought process to where they'll get money. Granted, if you don't have the money, it's normal to worry about where or how you'll get it. However, as we review some of the common sources of financing below, you'll realize that the most important thing is to understand the strings attached to each form of financing. In most cases, anyone who fronts you some money for your business will always want something in return. Let's explore your options:

Angel Investors

These are wealthy individuals who offer their capital to startups in exchange for equity ownership or convertible debt. Apart from offering capital, some angel investors could also support your business by offering valuable insight based on their experience in the industry. This kind of mentorship can help you navigate the challenges of entrepreneurship in the early days, making it easier to find your footing in the business. More importantly, you could also benefit from their connections and the strength of their network. Since angel investing is generally less formal compared to similar options like venture capital, you have a better chance of raising larger sums of money through this approach. That being said, angel investors generally fund your business in exchange for part ownership. While ownership dilution might not be a problem, you might have different visions for the future of your business, which *could* be a problem, especially in terms of decision making, and the approach to your strategic plans.

Bootstrapping

In this case, you're using your own money, or revenue earned from your other businesses to finance your new business. Your own money, in this case, could be your personal savings, credit cards, or if you've already set up the business, you reinvest profits.

Bootstrapping revolves around your own money, so you don't need to worry about equity or debt. On top of that, you're in complete control of your business, so you can steer it forward in line with your vision, unlike the situation we saw with angel investors.

Unfortunately, this approach is limited to the extent of your financial ability. There's only so much that you can do with the capital at your disposal. Besides, if you use this approach, you are exposing yourself to massive financial risks at a personal level, especially if the business fails. Ultimately, the fact that your potential is limited to the strength of your personal finances also limits your business growth potential.

Crowdfunding

The crowdfunding concept is quite simple—lots of people contributing small sums of money that ultimately raise the total amount you need for your business. Some of the most popular crowdfunding platforms online include Indiegogo and Kickstarter. These platforms allow you to raise funds through equity crowdfunding, rewards, or pre-selling your products.

Crowdfunding is ideal if you do not wish to cede equity in your business, because your benefactors contribute out of the goodness of their hearts. Apart from that, you also don't need to validate your product, or delve into the dynamics of your potential customer base. You simply make a pitch about your business, why you need funding, and anyone who feels moved by your story can chip in whatever they can. Unfortunately, this is one of the most time-consuming methods of financing, especially since you're relying on people's goodwill, without some of the checks and balances that come with formal funding schemes like venture capital and angel investing. You must also be socially responsible when you use this approach, because some investors do their due diligence before and after contributing to your cause, to ensure that their money is in the right place. Therefore, if your business fails, you could face serious backlash on social media and other online platforms.

Friends and Family

This is somewhat similar to crowdfunding, except that you're getting money from people who know you personally. Your friends and family contributing to your business can be such a confidence boost—proof that they believe in you, and are willing to go the extra mile for you. It's actually a common funding approach especially in the early stages of your business when you're setting up the foundation. Support could be in the form of equity investment, gifts, or loans.

Since these are people who know you and how hard you've worked for this dream, friends and family members can be some of the most supportive investors you'll ever bring into your business. If they offer loans, the terms are usually lower than market rates, with more flexibility on the repayment terms.

Unfortunately, the risks of this approach also come down to the personal nature of your relations. It's common knowledge that borrowing money from loved ones can strain your relationships, especially when things don't work out. Where equity is concerned, your personal differences could scupper your strategic plans for the business, with internal wrangles and other private matters interwoven into business decisions. Support from loved ones often does not include formal agreements, so it's based on mutual trust, which could also strain both your personal and business relationships over time. If this is your only option to raise money, your access to capital is limited to the overall net worth of your friends and family.

Grants and Government Programs

Many governments and non-profit organizations offer grants and funding programs to support small businesses, usually in specific industries or regions, so you should check with the local offices to find out what's available in your area. Apart from the fact that they are non-repayable, most businesses that apply for such programs get recognition from the participating organizations, which goes a long way in boosting your credibility. Unfortunately, these programs are fiercely contested, so you'll have to fend off stiff competition from other applicants. Since these grants are non-repayable, the requirements are often stringent, and in many cases, you also have strict reporting obligations to prove that the funds are used for the intended purpose.

Personal Savings and Assets

This is quite simple, you use your own savings or sell some personal assets to fund your business. You maintain full control over the business, and always have quick access to funds when you need them. Just like bootstrapping, this approach exposes you to serious personal financial risks in case things don't work out as you'd hoped. Similarly, the amount of capital you can raise through this approach is limited to your net worth.

Small Business Loans

Most people tend to shy away from small business loans, yet a lot of business owners swear by them. You can apply for a small business loan from online lenders, credit unions, or your bank. These loans accrue interest, so you need to ensure the interest isn't so high that it eats into your profits.

Unless you default on the loan and your lender initiates the recovery process stipulated in your loan agreement, you maintain full ownership of the business as long as you're servicing your loan according to your contractual obligation. Loans are also a decent option in terms of the potential tax benefits when filing your returns because they reduce your tax liability. Always read and understand the terms of the loan agreement, especially regarding the lender's recourse in case you cannot continue servicing the loan. Investors generally want assurances that they backed the right horse. Therefore, it would be wise to periodically send them updates on progress, milestones you've accomplished, and so on. For a new business, understand that your investors might be skeptical about your prospects, and for that reason, you must work hard to convince them your business was the perfect investment. Your prudence might even prompt some investors to front you more money to supercharge your growth, or even propose strategic partnerships or a direction to diversify your business prospects.

Basic Financial Management Skills

Once you've got the money you need for your business, the next step is how to effectively manage it. Don't let the money get into your head. This isn't free money, and depending on the source of funding, your investors might even own a stake in your business, which makes you answerable to them. This is about inspiring confidence in your investors, so the first thing you need to do is become an astute financial manager. Granted, financial management might not have been on your mind when you explored the idea of financial support, but this is where you are right now, and you cannot avoid it. For the record, this doesn't necessarily mean enrolling for a financial course, but if that works for you, then go for it, because the skills you learn will come in handy. When we talk about financial management and budgeting, in a nutshell, we're talking about your long-term success. Here are some simple tips to set you on the right path:

- Have a comprehensive business plan that outlines your short and long-term business goals, target market, revenue streams, and estimated expenses, which will become your financial roadmap.

- Open a dedicated business bank account so you don't mix personal and business finances. This should make it easier to track your business expenses and income.

- Use accounting software or hire a bookkeeper to accurately record and track all your business expenses.

- Create a realistic budget guided by your business plan, and regularly compare your actual expenses to your budget and adjust accordingly.

- Monitor your cash flow statements to ensure you have enough cash to cover your expenses.

- Always explore the prospect of cost-cutting without compromising quality. For example, you can negotiate better agreements with suppliers, consider discounts through bulk purchasing, or save costs by managing your social media marketing on your own.

- Understand your tax obligations and engage a tax attorney or an accountant to help you with tax laws and maximize deductions.

- Just like you do in your household, create an emergency fund for your business. This will help you through difficult periods, especially when the business is not doing so well.

- Pay attention to your financial statements to understand the financial health of your business, and help you make smart decisions.

- Engage professionals like mentors, accountants, and your financial advisor for deeper insight into the world of business, and to help you avoid common challenges that befall many businesses.

One of the most important lessons about business is that you must be flexible. Nothing is cast in stone, so you must embrace a growth mindset and learn to adapt to changing market conditions.

Advanced Tips

While the points above will mostly come in handy when you're starting a business, you have to think outside the box from time to time. If you've been in the business already, you understand the dynamics of funding and its challenges from experience. Whether you are setting up a new product line, a massive marketing drive ahead of the holidays, or for any other reason, here are some advanced strategies that you could implement to raise money for your business, which might not be feasible for beginners and startups:

- **Initial Coin Offerings (ICO)**

ICOs are a brilliant idea if you understand the dynamics of cryptocurrency, or blockchain technology in general. ICOs operate in more or less the same way as Initial Public Offerings (IPOs) for companies listed at the stock exchange. Instead of issuing stock in your business, you're issuing digital tokens.

Anyone who buys tokens in your ICO anticipates value appreciation as your business grows—there is a similar expectation with IPOs. Now, before you go this route, you must understand the regulatory and market risks involved in this process. What guarantees are you offering investors?

ICOs carry the risk of regulatory frameworks, because they're still a gray area as far as classification as a source of funding is concerned. Where regulation exists, it varies from one jurisdiction to the next, so you can't be sure of the regulatory position on the issuance and trade of tokens. This means that there's always a risk of penalties, fines, and legal action if your ICO contravenes the law of the land. Apart from that, if tokens are classified as securities, this would mean stringent requirements for compliance, which many small businesses cannot handle. The wider blockchain ecosystem is a vastly evolving space, so you cannot preempt the evolutionary path as far as regulation is concerned. Thus, if you choose to approach business funding from an ICO perspective, I'd advise you to consult an attorney, preferably one who understands blockchain technology.

- **Convertible Notes**

These are short-term debt instruments that you can convert into equity at a later date, typically during a future financing round. They are attractive to investors because they offer downside protection while offering the potential for equity upside. Convertible notes are ideal for startups especially if you need quick funding without immediately setting a valuation.

- **Revenue-Based Financing**

This is where you raise capital by agreeing to repay your investors with a percentage of future revenue. This method aligns investor returns with the performance of your business without diluting your ownership structure. Therefore, you remain in control of the business, unlike other methods where your investors own part of the business. You could consider this when setting up a business with predictable revenue streams and massive growth potential. After all, all you have to do is make sure your business is making profits.

- **Government Programs**

You could explore government programs like grants, subsidies, and low-interest loans to support innovation, research and development, and job creation. These funds do not require equity or repayment, making them highly attractive, and are available at federal, state, and local levels, so keep an eye out for opportunities relevant to your industry and location.

- **Strategic Partnerships**

This might be a difficult one, but try to approach established businesses and discuss the prospect of getting funding, resources, or access to their markets. If successful, they could invest in your startup in exchange for a stake or other strategic benefits. This approach can only work when there are clear synergies between your business and the partner you're approaching. Basically, you have to come to the table with something valuable for a potential partner to consider your proposal.

- **Equity Crowdfunding**

This is different from crowdfunding, which we discussed earlier, in that your investors acquire ownership stakes in your business. You can explore this in Platforms like SeedInvest and Crowdcube. The concept remains the same, helping you to raise significant capital from a large pool of investors. Through equity crowdfunding, you're not just getting support, but investors also have access to unique investment opportunities in diverse markets.

- **Family Offices**

Family offices, which manage the investments of high-net-worth families, tend to explore and invest in startups. Due to their valuation, such families can provide substantial funding and on top of that, they could be more flexible and patient than traditional venture capitalists as you build your business from the ground-up. The beauty of this approach is that if they love your idea, you won't just get financial support, you might also enjoy strategic support from your financiers. Depending on the nature of your proposal, some families might even embrace you just as they would their actual family members.

Chapter 4:

Building Your Brand

You've figured a way around the funding problem, and have the finances necessary according to your business plan. In essence, you're good to go. Your next step is how to build a brand. There are names that automatically come to mind when you think of something—that's how branding should be. For example, when we talk about social media, Facebook and Instagram are some of the first platforms most people think about. If you talk about smartphones, most people will instantly think of either Samsung or iPhone. Talk about web browsers, and you can be certain Google Chrome is one of the first, as is Gmail in email service providers.

While there are lots of other brands in the categories that we've mentioned, and most of them are quite successful, customers instantly think of the brands we mentioned, and for a good reason. These brands are ever present in the customers' space. They've all had their fair share of ups and downs, but they constantly deliver on the promise they made to their customers.

People don't care that Google Chrome has had a series of hacks and exploits in the past, because they know they can still rely on it as an efficient web browser. This shows you how far customers are willing to go for you if you can give them something they want, and be consistent at doing so.

Brand building for your new business is a crucial step in establishing your presence in the market, and encouraging customer loyalty. You need an effective brand story to build a brand image that resonates with consumers on an emotional level. A brand story is a cohesive narrative that highlights the facts and feelings created by your brand. Unlike traditional advertising that focuses on presenting products or services, your brand story specifically evokes emotions and creates a memorable experience.

A brand story for your business is important for the following reasons:

- People remember stories more than they remember facts or figures. A compelling brand story can create an emotional bond with your audience.

- In a crowded market, a unique brand story can set your brand apart from competitors.

- A strong brand story fosters trust and loyalty as customers feel connected to the brand's mission and values.

- It provides a consistent theme for all marketing and communication efforts, ensuring a unified brand message.

- Internally, a brand story can inspire and motivate your employees, making it easier for them to align with your company's vision and mission.

Creating a Brand Identity

Creating an identity for your business that customers can easily relate to requires a unique understanding of the product or service features, values, and visual elements that set it apart from competitors. To do that, you must also match your intended brand vision with knowledge of your customer demographics. For example:

- Who are your target customers?

- What do they like about the competitor?

- How can you persuade them to choose your brand over the competition?

- What's the general nature of the market?

This foundational analysis informs the development of a brand strategy that aligns with your company's goals and, at the same time, meets the needs of your customers. It's also a way to clearly articulate what your brand stands for, and once you can do that, go on to establish a strong identity that fosters recognition and loyalty.

How cohesive is your brand? This is purely about design. Consider your preferred colors, logo design, typography, and other visual elements such as imagery and graphics. If you're not artistic, work with an expert, or even a freelancer to create these for you. The goal here is to create an element of consistency in your brand, reflecting your brand's personality and values across all platforms. A well-designed visual identity will enhance brand recognition and also help to convey your brand's message to your audience effectively.

A cohesive brand is not limited to the visuals. It's also about the tone and voice in which you communicate with your audience. The way you engage customers through written content, social media interactions, or customer service, should be consistent and align with your overall image. For example, what voice do you want to portray in your brand? Are you looking for a professional, friendly, innovative, or authoritative tone? Just like the visuals, your tone must also be consistent across all platforms to build trust in your customers.

Your brand identity goes beyond design and communication to include customer experience. Every interaction a customer has with your brand, from website navigation to product packaging and customer service, contributes to their overall perception of your business. You should regularly review and refine these elements to maintain consistency with your brand identity.

Finally, creating a brand identity is an ongoing process that requires regular evaluation and adaptation. As market conditions, consumer preferences, and business objectives evolve, you must also be flexible and willing to adjust your identity where necessary to stay relevant. This means that you should be open to the idea of rebranding, which can include tweaking some visual elements, redefining your brand message, or even repositioning your products or services in the market. In the long run, your business will only be relevant in the market if you are proactive in how you manage your brand identity.

Building Brand Awareness

Once you've figured out the dynamics of your brand, from the visuals to the message you wish to convey to your customers, the next step is how to make them aware of your existence. Brand awareness refers to the strategic steps you take to ensure your target customers recognize and remember your brand. By understanding what sets your brand apart, you can effectively communicate this to your audience. This clarity in branding forms the foundation for all your awareness-building activities.

The next step is to leverage multiple marketing channels to reach a broader audience. This includes traditional media such as print, television, and radio where possible, as well as digital platforms like social media, email marketing, and your website. Each platform has its strengths, and a diversified approach allows you to tap into different audience categories. Social media, for instance, is ideal for building brand awareness through engaging content, influencer partnerships, and targeted advertising.

Once again, I have to stress the need for consistency in your branding across whichever platforms you intend to use. This means using the same logo, brand colors, tone, and messaging across all your marketing efforts. Consistency helps reinforce your identity, making it easier for your audience to recognize your brand. With this recognition, you also build a brand customers can trust. Note, however, that trust is earned, and this is only possible in your business practices.

Engaging with your audience is another key aspect of building brand awareness. It takes anything from interactive content like surveys, quizzes, or contests to achieve this. Simple things like responding to comments and messages on social media go a long way in creating the desired narrative for your audience. You could also consider personalized email marketing campaigns that address the specific needs and interests of your customers. Ideally, brand awareness through engagement is about creating a two-way communication channel where you help your customers feel valued and heard.

All this effort is futile if you cannot identify what's working and what's not. Track all the relevant brand awareness metrics, for example website traffic, social media engagement, and conversion rates. Analyzing them to understand what strategies are working and where there is room for improvement. Review and adjust your strategies accordingly to ensure your approach is effective and aligned with your overall business goals.

Marketing on a Budget

If you're on a budget, marketing calls for strategic planning and creativity to maximize the impact of your efforts without substantial financial investment. Here are some simple tips to build an effective marketing strategy without breaking the bank:

- **Capitalize on Social Media**

Social media is one of the most cost-effective solutions to reaching and engaging with your audience. Establishing a presence on Facebook, Instagram, Twitter, and LinkedIn allows you to connect with potential customers through organic posts, stories, and community engagement. Consistently posting relevant content, sharing user-generated content, and participating in conversations can significantly enhance your brand's visibility. Besides, there are lots of free analytics tools on these platforms that can help you understand what content works best with your audience.

- **Content Marketing**

If you want to attract and retain customers, consider content marketing. Valuable and informative content like blog posts, videos, infographics, and eBooks, can give your brand an authority image in your industry. Engagement from content marketing will help you drive organic traffic to your website, and in the process, also build trust and credibility with your customers. Always optimize your content for better performance on search engines to improve your rankings and increase visibility. Be proactive, and publish high-quality content regularly to attract a loyal audience.

- **Email Marketing**

While most customers prefer social media engagement, email marketing is equally effective, especially if you're targeting customers who like formal communication. One thing you'll appreciate about email marketing is that it's direct. By building and maintaining a mailing list, you can send targeted campaigns that promote your products, share news, or offer exclusive deals. There are lots of tools, like Mailchimp, that even have free plans for small businesses, making it easy to design and send professional emails. Consider personalizing your message to enhance the effectiveness of your email campaigns, and ensure that your messages are relevant to each recipient.

- **Collaborate with Influencers and Partners**

Partnering with influencers or other businesses can expand your reach without a significant financial outlay. Micro-influencers, who have smaller but highly engaged audiences, are often more affordable and can provide authentic endorsements of your brand. You can also reach out to businesses whose products or services are complementary to yours, for co-marketing initiatives. Using this approach, you can set up joint webinars, giveaways, or content sharing to reach new audiences. These partnerships are beneficial for each participating brand.

- **Utilize Free and Low-Cost Tools**

There are lots of free or affordable marketing tools available online that can help streamline your efforts and enhance your marketing strategy. Tools like Canva for graphic design, Hootsuite for social media management, Google Analytics for website analytics, and Buffer for content scheduling are excellent resources that add value to your marketing efficiency. With these tools, you can create professional marketing materials, schedule posts, monitor performance, and optimize your campaigns on a budget.

Sales Strategies for Beginners

You have to be practical when designing your sales strategy. For example, instead of posting content on social media randomly, take some notes on what you want to achieve and how. What product or service are you promoting, and at what time? Timing is important, especially since you need to get your customers' attention at the perfect time to capitalize on exposure. What's your unique selling point? What makes your product or service better than those of your competitors?

With this knowledge, you can then come up with a marketing strategy that effectively captures the value you're presenting to potential customers. On top of that, your content will be more enjoyable because you present a confident brand that customers find credible, and persuasive.

Knowledge of your target market is crucial for your sales strategy. You must define who your ideal customers are, including their demographics, needs, and pain points. By understanding your target audience, you can tailor your sales pitch to address their specific concerns and interests. This targeted approach increases the likelihood of addressing their needs effectively, and turning potential customers into buyers. Consider creating different buyer personas to gain more insight into your customers' preferences and behavior.

One of the most underrated elements of marketing and sales is building relationships with your customers. Relationships are built on trust. Customers trust that your business will meet their needs effectively, while you trust that your customers will walk the journey with you, buy from you and recommend your business within their networks. While it is a mutually beneficial arrangement, you have to make the first move, and show your customers why they should work with you instead of your competitors. Focus on creating genuine connections with your prospects by actively listening to their needs and providing relevant solutions. Trust and rapport with your customers can lead to long-term relationships and repeat business. Relationship-building not only enhances customer satisfaction but will equally encourage word-of-mouth referrals, which are valuable for expanding your customer base.

For a first-time business owner, consultative selling is one approach that can make a big difference for you. This is a situation where you act as an advisor or consultant rather than a salesperson. Use CRM tools to track and manage your interactions with customers, providing valuable insight into their behavior and motives behind their purchase decisions.

Remember, sales is a dynamic aspect of your business, so you must constantly revise and adjust your sales strategy. Don't just engage customers when they like your posts, but reach out to the loyal ones to learn their perspectives on various aspects of your strategy. You can even invite them to be your brand ambassadors. Whichever approach you use, never rest easy. Even if a strategy is working for you today, there's always room for improvement.

Advanced Tips

Building a strong brand requires advanced strategies that go beyond the basics of logo design and social media presence. To truly differentiate your brand and create lasting impact, consider implementing the following advanced tips:

- **Develop a Strong Brand Narrative**

A compelling brand narrative weaves your mission, values, and unique selling propositions into a cohesive story that resonates with your audience. Craft a narrative that highlights your brand's journey, challenges, and triumphs, and connects emotionally with your customers. This story should be consistently communicated across all platforms and marketing materials, creating a memorable and relatable brand identity. A strong narrative not only attracts attention but also fosters deep emotional connections and loyalty among your audience.

- **Invest in Customer Experience**

Exceptional customer experience (CX) is a key differentiator for advanced brand building. Every interaction a customer has with your brand, from the first touchpoint to post-purchase support, should be seamless, personalized, and memorable. Invest in technology and training to ensure that your customer service is responsive and empathetic. Implementing CRM systems and leveraging customer feedback can help you tailor experiences to individual preferences. By exceeding customer expectations, you can turn satisfied customers into brand advocates who willingly promote your brand.

- **Cultivate Brand Ambassadors**

Brand ambassadors are influential customers or employees who passionately advocate for your brand. Identify and nurture relationships with individuals who genuinely love your products or services and have the credibility to influence others. Encourage and support these ambassadors by providing them with exclusive access, special perks, and opportunities to share their experiences. Authentic endorsements from trusted individuals can significantly enhance your brand's credibility and reach, particularly in today's social media-driven landscape.

Chapter 5:

Financial Management

Many small businesses and startups fail because of improper financial management. This is quite an unfortunate predicament because most of these businesses struggled to raise the funds to set up operations in the first place. That's why in Chapter 3, we discussed some smart ways of financing your startup, just in case you don't have the money to bankroll your business plan. Now, imagine all the meetings you took to convince potential investors to buy into your idea, the rejections, the long hours you put into creating proposals, only for your business to collapse because you don't know how to manage your finances. That's such a bummer, right?

When you're passionate about something like your business, you go the extra mile to make sure everything runs smoothly. That's why it's important to take financial management seriously. Contrary to what most people believe, you don't need a degree in accounting or finance to run an astute business. Having that knowledge will be a bonus, but it's not mandatory.

Effective financial management is crucial for the survival and growth of your business. From the onset, you need to establish a robust financial plan that outlines your revenue streams, operating costs, and projected profits. This plan will not only guide your daily financial decisions but also provide a clear roadmap for scaling your business. Having such a plan helps you allocate resources efficiently, ensuring that every dollar spent contributes to your strategic goals and long-term sustainability.

As a startup, your cash flow might be irregular and unpredictable. You must monitor your cash inflows and outflows meticulously to avoid liquidity crises that could jeopardize your operations. This involves managing accounts receivable and payable effectively, maintaining a cash reserve for emergencies, and forecasting future cash needs. By doing so, you can ensure that your business remains solvent and can meet its financial obligations promptly. Furthermore, proof of sound financial management will come in handy when seeking external funding. Investors and lenders require comprehensive and accurate financial statements to assess your startup's viability and growth potential. Demonstrating strong financial management practices can increase your chances of securing the necessary capital. For example, you must maintain detailed financial records, prepare regular financial reports, and be transparent about your financial health. This will help you build trust with different stakeholders and position your startup as a reliable investment.

One crucial aspect of financial management is that as you learn the ropes of the business, you also learn how to identify and mitigate risks beforehand. The business environment is quite volatile, with numerous uncertainties. It's important to learn how to analyze your financial data and identify trends and potential issues before they escalate. With this proactive approach, you can adjust your strategies, cut unnecessary expenses, and optimize your operations to keep your business in better financial health. Ultimately, diligent financial management empowers you to navigate challenges effectively and capitalize on opportunities, ensuring the long-term success of your business.

Establish Financial Goals and Budget

What do you want to achieve financially? What are your goals? Your goals should always inform your budget and every other financial decision you make. Clear financial goals set the strategic direction and measurable targets to aim for. They guide your efforts and resources on achieving specific financial outcomes, such as reaching a certain revenue milestone, profitability, or expanding into new markets. Once you define clear objectives you can track your progress, make smart decisions, and adjust your strategies accordingly.

Budgeting is equally important because it keeps you in check, helps you plan and manage resources effectively, and makes sure your funds are allocated accordingly. A good budget ensures that your business has sufficient capital to cover essential expenses while also investing in growth opportunities. When you follow your budget accordingly, you stay in control over your expenditure, avoid unnecessary debt, and maintain a healthy cash flow. It is this kind of disciplined approach to financial management that helps you avoid overspending and makes sure your startup remains financially stable.

A careful balance between your budget and financial goals sets the perfect framework for evaluating your startup's performance. For evaluation, you will compare the actual financial results against your budget and goals to identify variances and understand the reasons behind them. Once you do that, you can easily identify areas where you may need to make some changes to ensure your financial plans are not derailed.

Staying within your budget and the confines of your financial goals makes it easier to engage stakeholders, especially your financiers, and help them see the bigger picture. Investors generally want assurances that putting their money in your business was a smart move. This calls for responsible financial management, which in the long run influences your ability to plan for the future.

Cash Flow Management

Cash flow management is another important step in budgeting and financial management because it directly determines how well your business is doing. In the previous section, we highlighted the role of budgeting, especially guided by your financial goals. Cash flow management is a crucial part of this because it shows you how money is moving in the business.

For first-time businesses, it's easy to get overwhelmed by various challenges that arise from time to time. However, if you have a clear view of what comes in and out of the business, you should have an easier time managing your finances.

Here are some essential considerations for effectively managing cash flow:

- **Forecasting**

Start by creating detailed cash flow projections for the upcoming weeks or months. Make realistic assumptions of your expected incomes and expenditures over the period in question. While it's not possible to make accurate predictions, you can make smart guesses based on the information at your disposal. With this, it's easier to assess possible cash shortages and take appropriate measures to save the situation.

- **Monitoring Cash Flow**

Apart from the forecasts, pay attention to the actual movement of money through the business. Track your income and expenses on a daily basis. Have weekly and monthly reviews and compare these with the forecasts you made earlier. Are your projections in line with the actual situation? Be vigilant and identify outliers, possible issues you might not have anticipated, and take corrective action before they escalate into serious problems.

While at it, keep a close eye on your expenses and look for opportunities to reduce costs without sacrificing quality or efficiency. Explore the possibility of eliminating non-essential expenses, or finding more cost-effective alternatives for certain products or services.

- **Managing Accounts Receivable**

Be proactive when invoicing customers and follow up on overdue payments to ensure they are not left pending for a long time. The longer customers stay with unpaid invoices, the stronger the chokehold on your business. You might also want to consider offering incentives for early payments or implementing stricter credit policies to minimize the risk of late or unpaid invoices.

- **Negotiating Payment Terms**

When dealing with suppliers or creditors, try to negotiate favorable payment terms that do not interfere with your cash flow cycle. For example, you may request extended payment terms or staggered payments to alleviate short-term cash constraints.

- **Reinvesting Wisely**

While it's tempting to reinvest all profits back into the business for growth, you need to decide which is the smarter option between reinvesting the money and maintaining adequate cash reserves. Evaluate all investment opportunities carefully and prioritize those that provide the highest return on investment while also considering their impact on your cash flow.

Cash flow management is about making sure there's enough money flowing in the business to keep things running smoothly. If you are ever at a point where you need external financial support, weigh your options carefully. Every line of credit you explore comes with unique strains on your cash flow, so consider all the risks and potential costs involved before making such decisions.

Be proactive and set aside some money to build an emergency cash reserve. This will be your backup plan in the event of unexpected downturns in the market, or unforeseen expenses. If anything, the emergency reserve should be a part of your financial plan, where you set aside a portion of your profits to build a safety net for your business.

Debt Management

Debt is a normal part of business. Even the most successful brands like Samsung, NVIDIA, and Tesla operate with some level of debt on their books. This is because debt allows businesses to thrive without necessarily committing their own finances. We call this leverage, where you use someone else's money to fund your projects, and spread the costs over a number of years. To effectively manage debt as a startup, you must be smart in your approach to financial decisions. Start by assessing how much debt your startup can reasonably manage in the current financial environment. Consider your growth plans and revenue projections in this assessment so you don't end up taking on more debt than your business can comfortably afford to repay. Remember, just because your bank is willing to loan you some money, doesn't necessarily mean you need it, or can afford it. Excessive and unreasonable debt will strain your cash flow and hinder your ability to grow. Here are some key steps to consider:

- **Shop Around for the Best Terms**

If you have to take out a loan, explore various lending options to find the most favorable terms and interest rates. Compare offers from different lenders, including banks, credit unions, online lenders, and government-backed loan programs. Negotiate terms that suit your business goals and ability to repay.

- **Use Debt Wisely**

Be strategic in how you use borrowed funds, focusing on investments that generate positive returns and contribute to your business's growth and profitability. Try as much as possible not to borrow money to cover operating expenses or fund unnecessary expenses that don't provide a clear benefit to your business.

Before you borrow money, make sure you have a solid repayment plan. A good plan outlines how you'll repay debts, taking into consideration factors like the interest rates, repayment terms, and cash flow projections.

- **Communicate with Lenders**

Once you borrow some money, engage your creditors and lenders and keep the lines of communication open at all times. This is particularly important if you realize you might have a difficult time meeting your debt obligations. Be transparent about your situation and proactive in addressing any issues that arise.

Many lenders are willing to work with you to find mutually beneficial solutions. For example, they could restructure your debt or adjust your repayment terms to accommodate your new financial position.

I would also encourage you to prioritize paying down your debts whenever possible to reduce interest costs and improve your financial health. If possible, allocate any excess cash flow or profits toward debt repayment, and always start with high-interest debt or loans with unfavorable terms.

Finally, familiarize yourself with the tax laws and regulations that apply to your business at the local, state, and federal levels. Each jurisdiction may have specific requirements and deadlines for filing taxes, reporting income, and paying applicable taxes such as income tax, sales tax, payroll tax, and excise tax. Stay updated on any changes to tax laws that may affect your business, and seek professional guidance if needed to ensure compliance.

Engage professionals like tax advisors, accountants, or tax attorneys who specialize in startup taxation and can provide expert guidance according to your specific needs and circumstances. Investing in professional tax services can save you time, money, and potential legal consequences in the long run, allowing you to focus on growing your business.

Chapter 6:

Overcome Common Startup Challenges

Starting a business might seem like a difficult task, but I can guarantee you that's not it. If anything, the biggest challenge any entrepreneur has to overcome is keeping the business alive. Think of this like buying a car. The fact that you have the money to pay for it in cash doesn't mean you can afford it. Keeping that car on the road every day, well-maintained, serviced, and fueled is what determines whether you can afford it.

The same concept applies to your business. Sure, you managed to raise funds and got it up and running. Keeping it open in the face of stiff competition, and many other obstacles that you will encounter is where the hard work begins. In this chapter, we'll address common challenges that businesses face from time to time, giving you insight on how to overcome them and keep your business afloat. The goal is to answer the following questions by the end of this chapter:

- How do I enter a new market?

- How can I compete against established brands?

- How do I survive a market that's constantly evolving?

The challenges you face will test your resolve and ingenuity. Since your business is already running, you've probably found a way around one of the biggest obstacles—funding! Convincing investors to back your vision can be a daunting task, especially when you're competing with numerous other startups for attention and resources. You might not realize it yet, but you've already accomplished more than most, so congratulations!

Competition

Competition is part of the game. It encourages innovation as each business tries to outdo the other. For a startup, it can be difficult going up against established businesses. I mean, they already have the customer base, yet you're trying to find your footing. Beyond customer loyalty, they might also have the resources, and brand recognition, putting more pressure on you. Well, don't despair. First, try to understand your competitors, so you know what you're up against.

Thorough market research should help you understand who your competitors are, what they offer, and their strengths and weaknesses. This could give you insight into market gaps and opportunities you can exploit in the market. From that, it gets easier to create a unique value proposition that sets your product or service apart. Yours might not be superior, but just good enough to get people talking. The goal here is to stand out in a crowded market.

Have you considered niche marketing? Instead of trying to capture the entire market, target a specific niche where you can establish a strong presence. Concentrate your efforts and resources on a segment that is underserved or overlooked by larger competitors. In the process, you'll also be building strong customer relationships and brand loyalty. Rest assured that every market served by large companies always has dissatisfied customers who long for the good old days when they could get personalized attention from the brands they love. Exploit such opportunities.

Finally, when you're going up against established competitors, you must be prepared to adapt your business model and strategies in response to market changes and competitive actions. Be proactive. That's how you remain relevant in a highly competitive space.

Barriers to Market Entry

Gatekeeping has denied many entrepreneurs the opportunity to realize their dreams, with ridiculous barriers to entry making it harder to launch or grow your business. These barriers can take various forms, including high initial capital requirements, stringent regulatory requirements, established brand dominance, or even limited access to distribution channels. Most of these issues usually come up during the research stage, so you can preempt them and find smart workarounds to smoothen your entry into the industry.

In some cases, you might have an easier entry through strategic partnerships with companies that are already established in the industry. Such arrangements can provide you with access to distribution networks, shared resources, and industry expertise, which give you an easier entry into the industry compared to what you would have had to go through on your own.

Whether you get in through partnerships or not, you must innovate from the very beginning. Innovate to differentiate your product or service from what's in the market. Unique features, superior quality, or any other innovative solutions should address unmet needs in the market, especially since you've already done your research on the competition and understand where they are falling short. Despite the presence of dominant brands, an innovative entry can help you carve out a niche and attract customers.

Another area where you must innovate is your costing strategy. Look for ways to minimize costs without compromising quality. You could outsource some functions, leverage technology to streamline operations, or adopt lean startup principles to maximize resource efficiency.

Ideally, you need to create a comprehensive plan that outlines how you will enter the market, attract customers, and achieve growth, taking into consideration the different barriers that you might face. Your strategy must include plans for marketing, distribution, sales, and even customer experience.

Build a Strong Team

Your team will make or break your vision for the business. As far as obstacles go, this should be an easy one because it's in your control. Granted, you might have some brilliant ideas for your business, but that does not mean you have the know-how to find people with the right skills and expertise. This is where many entrepreneurs get it wrong. The worst thing about this predicament is that it rears its ugly head right when you're exploring the prospect of scaling up operations.

If hiring or vetting potential employees is not your strongest skill, outsource this to professionals. Make sure you share with them your company culture and mission so they know what to look for in candidates. Candidates who resonate with your company's ethos are more likely to be motivated and committed. Besides, limited resources, a competitive job market, and the need for diverse skill sets can easily complicate this task, hence the need to outsource it. If you go that route, your hiring managers should be able to present your business as a positive and dynamic work environment.

Define the roles you need to fill and the specific skills and qualifications required for each position. This clarity will help you attract candidates who are well-suited to your needs and can contribute effectively from day one. Research well to understand the kind of benefits and compensation that aligns with these roles. Even with limited resources, try to offer competitive salaries and benefits to attract top talent.

Once you have the right people in the company, continuously assess your team structure and adapt accordingly. Be prepared to scale your team by adding new roles and responsibilities, and by bringing in specialists or managers to support expanding operations. Create opportunities for training and development to help your team members grow their skills, improve performance, and when done properly, reduce turnover, which essentially strengthens their loyalty to your cause.

Stress and Burnout

Being an entrepreneur is one of the most challenging roles in the world. It's even harder if you're doing it alone. You're responsible for everything from financing, strategy, and marketing, to the day-to-day running of your business. This can be a tall order, and could end up in stress and burnout. The high demands and fast-paced nature of building a new business don't make things any easier either. As you work to establish your startup, the pressure to meet deadlines, achieve milestones, and manage limited resources can lead to long hours and intense stress. This can negatively affect both your well-being and overall productivity. Even though entrepreneurs are some of the most overworked people, this doesn't have to be your fate. Start by championing a healthy work-life balance for yourself and your team. Set clear boundaries between work and personal time, and encourage regular breaks for people to recharge. If possible, consider flexible working hours, and remote or hybrid work options.

While the can-do attitude is a good thing, it can also lead you down an unfortunate rabbit hole where you take on too many tasks. Know when to take a break, especially if you're working alone. If you have a team, delegate responsibilities according to individual strengths and expertise. While at it, try to create achievable goals and milestones for your startup so you don't put everyone under pressure over unattainable goals. Break down large projects into smaller, manageable tasks to maintain a steady progress pace and reduce the overwhelming feeling that often leads to stress.

Health and wellness programs can make a big difference for yourself and your team. Be the kind of employer who promotes physical and mental well-being, with things like wellness workshops, mental health resources, meditation sessions, or if you can afford it, gym memberships. If you do that, you'll easily attract top talent. More importantly, set the right examples for your team to follow. You cannot encourage people to take time off when you never seem to catch a breather yourself. As a leader, set an example by managing your stress levels to avoid burnout.

Demonstrate healthy work habits, such as taking breaks, managing your workload, and maintaining a positive attitude. Your behavior sets a standard for your team to follow.

Dynamic Market

If there's one thing we've learned from the AI explosion it's that change is always imminent. In business, you either adapt or perish. The fact that most industries are so dynamic presents a significant challenge to startups. You're always on your toes, trying to stay ahead of rapid changes in consumer preferences, technological advancements, and pressure from competitors. While this is a good thing for the entrepreneurial spirit, the unpredictability forces you into constant adaptation and agility. A dynamic market can disrupt your business plans, making it difficult to achieve stability and growth, especially if you're always playing catch-up. One solution for this is to invest in extensive and ongoing market research. Regularly analyze market data and gather customer feedback. This can help you understand changes in demand and customer preferences, and make relevant adjustments to stay competitive.

Flexibility is mandatory in every industry, so you can quickly adapt to changes. Even within your team, encourage an innovative culture where your employees feel comfortable and free to share ideas, to pivot strategies that can give you an edge in the market. Being flexible also means keeping a close eye on your competitors' activities and strategies. You have to try and preempt or, at the very least, understand their moves to get valuable insights into the state of the industry and help you anticipate market shifts.

Advanced Tips

When it comes to obstacles and challenges in your business, you must think outside the box, always. That's one skill that sets you apart from other businesses, and will certainly take you places. Having discussed some simple strategies to get you through everyday challenges, let's explore some advanced strategies, especially for people who've been in the business for a while and have already figured a way around everyday problems:

- **Regulatory Compliance**

Engage legal experts in your industry to help you understand and navigate regulatory requirements. Be proactive on regulatory changes and adjust your business practices accordingly.

- **Securing Funding**

Whether you're a beginner or have years of experience in the business, money will always be a problem. No matter how well your business is running, for some reason there's never enough money for every project in your pipeline. Even if you have the money to commit to a project, you'll still have other obligations, so putting all the money in a single project is not advisable. This is why you must learn how to use leverage.

Leverage basically means using debt to pivot your project or investment. You can do that from banks and other financial institutions, or any other source of financing that's relevant to your situation. Engage with mentors, advisors, and other entrepreneurs who can introduce you to potential investors. In these discussions, make sure you can demonstrate clear metrics of growth, customer acquisition, and market validation to prove your business potential. More importantly, customize your pitch to align with the interests and portfolio of each potential investor.

- **Product-Market Fit**

Make a point of engaging customers directly from time to time to understand their pain points and refine your product accordingly. Go beyond the usual reviews and ask customers for specific information on what they'd like to see you do differently. You can even invite some customers to be part of your testing phase for a new product or service. With a lean startup approach, you can test hypotheses with minimal viable products (MVPs) and iterate based on that feedback.

- **Scaling Operations**

Save time and resources by innovating and automating processes where possible. As you streamline repetitive tasks, you free up time and resources, making it easier to focus on strategic initiatives—for example, developing and documenting your standard operating procedures (SOPs) to ensure consistency and efficiency as the business grows.

Chapter 7:

Growth and Scaling

Growth should always be at the back of your mind when you own a business. Growth is how you go from a sole proprietorship to hiring hundreds of employees some years down the line. This is a visionary approach to business that many entrepreneurs take for granted, missing massive opportunities to get good value for their money.

Growth and scalability go hand in hand. From scratch, build a business that has scalable potential. Weigh the advantages of scaling operations from the very beginning, and factor them into your overall business strategy. Planning for growth and scalability will help you anticipate future demand, streamline your business processes, and readjust your resources accordingly.

If you start your business with a vision of growing into something bigger, you already have an edge over some competitors because your thought process shifts to building a dynamic business that evolves with the needs and preferences of your customers and the prevailing market conditions.

Growth Objectives

Where do you want to see your business some years from now? What kind of customers are out of your reach right now but could be a part of your business in the future? What markets would you wish to invest in in down the road? These are some examples of questions that can help you explore growth prospects for your business from its early days.

When setting objectives for business growth, adopt a structured approach that aligns with your vision. Assess your current position, including your market position, finances, and operational capabilities. Analyze various aspects of your business, for example, market trends, competitors, financial statements, and operational processes to establish a clear growth strategy. Your growth objectives should contribute to your overall business goals and be actionable, and then make sure they meet the SMART criteria:

- Specific—Clearly define what you want to achieve.

- Measurable—Establish quantifiable metrics to track progress.

- Achievable—Set realistic goals that are within your reach.

- Relevant—Ensure objectives align with your business's mission and vision.

- Time-bound—Set deadlines to create a sense of urgency and accountability.

What are Your KPIs?

Key Performance Indicators (KPIs) are vital metrics that provide actionable insights into the performance of your business. By selecting the right KPIs, you gain a deeper understanding of your operations, and can make informed decisions to drive growth. Try to identify KPIs that provide meaningful benchmarks for success.

For example, if your objective is to increase sales revenue, you must track KPIs such as total sales volume, average transaction value, and sales growth rate. These metrics provide insight into the effectiveness of your sales strategies, emerging trends, and possible adjustments to optimize performance.

Similarly, if your goal is to enhance operational efficiency, KPIs such as production cycle time, inventory turnover ratio, and employee productivity can help identify areas for improvement. You can identify bottlenecks, streamline processes, and optimize resource allocation to drive efficiency gains. Beyond the KPIs, you'll also need to consider the resources and strategies necessary to achieve your growth objectives. Conduct a thorough analysis of your current capabilities and future needs. Evaluate both tangible resources, such as financial capital, technology, and physical infrastructure, as well as intangible assets like human capital, expertise, and brand reputation. From this assessment, you can identify gaps and areas of strength, develop a strategic plan to allocate resources effectively and support your growth initiatives.

Optimize Business Processes

Your growth strategy culminates in optimal business processes, focusing on enhancing efficiency, effectiveness, and adaptability. Start with a comprehensive review of your current processes, identifying areas where improvements can be made to streamline operations. This process is necessary for the following reasons:

- Reduces wasted time and resources, improving productivity and operational efficiency.

- Lowers operating costs, boosting profitability and competitiveness in the market.

- Generates better and consistent output, enhancing product or service quality and customer satisfaction.

- Adjusts to changing market conditions, seize opportunities, and mitigate risks.

Ideally, well-optimized processes set the foundation for scalable growth, making it easier for you to expand your operations without sacrificing quality or efficiency. One approach is to map out your existing processes, step by step, to gain a clear understanding of how tasks are performed and where bottlenecks may occur. This allows you to pinpoint areas for optimization to improve consistency and reliability.

Next, consider process improvements based on their potential impact on business performance and your strategic objectives. Assess the cost-benefit ratio of each proposed change and consider factors such as resource requirements, implementation complexity, and anticipated outcomes.

Once you've identified areas for improvement, implement changes gradually, monitoring their impact on key performance metrics like productivity and customer satisfaction. This approach allows you to test different solutions, gather feedback from stakeholders, and fine-tune processes to achieve better results.

Expand Products or Service Offerings

Scaling up operations requires a strategic approach that balances innovation with operational efficiency, particularly when you're expanding your product or service range. Why should you even be thinking about expansion yet you're just setting up your business?

- A diverse range allows your startup to meet the evolving needs and preferences of customers, enhancing your competitiveness and relevance in the market.

- Introducing new offerings can open up additional revenue streams, increasing your sales potential and overall profitability.

- Expansion allows you to attract new customers and retain existing ones by providing a broader range of solutions to their needs.

- Offering unique or innovative products or services sets your startup apart from competitors, helping to differentiate your brand and attract attention in a crowded marketplace.

- Diversifying your offerings can facilitate scalable growth by enabling you to tap into new markets or customer segments, spreading risk and reducing dependence on any single product or service.

- Continuously expanding and refining your offerings encourages a culture of innovation within your startup, fostering creativity and adaptability in response to changing market conditions.

First, research the market to identify emerging trends, customer needs, and competitive opportunities. This analysis will inform your decision-making process and guide the development of new offerings that align with market demand. Make sure your expansion efforts are driven by tangible factors like market potential, resource availability, and strategic fit with your existing business model. Invest in infrastructure and resources to support your expansion—for example technology upgrades or talent acquisition. Reallocate existing resources if possible, or seek strategic partnerships to access specialized expertise or resources.

As soon as your growth plan is in place, launch an aggressive marketing and sales campaign to promote your new offerings and attract customers. This may include targeted advertising campaigns, promotional discounts, or partnerships with influencers or distributors to expand your reach and generate awareness. Gather feedback from customers and stakeholders to identify areas for improvement as soon as the new offerings are in the market.

Explore Strategic Partnerships

Before engaging other businesses or brands as partners, ask yourself what you both stand to gain from the venture. This is important because the other business owner will want to know what value you bring to the table, for them to share their strategic position in the market with you. Strategic partnerships can give you access to resources, expertise, and opportunities that may not be available internally. By working with other businesses, you can easily leverage complementary strengths and capabilities, expand your reach and accelerate your growth in the market. One key benefit of strategic partnerships is access to new markets or customer segments. Partners who have established networks or distribution channels make it easier for you to penetrate new markets and reach a broader audience. Thus, such an arrangement can deliver increased sales and grow your market share without the need for significant investment in infrastructure or marketing, which you would have had to invest in if you did it all alone.

Besides, you'll also have access to specialized expertise or resources that may be necessary for scaling up your operations, which might have worked well for your partner. I'm talking about access to technology, intellectual property, manufacturing capabilities, or industry knowledge that your business may lack. As long as you work with entities that already have these capabilities, you can fill gaps in your own expertise and accelerate the development and delivery of new products or services.

I'd encourage you to consider such partnerships carefully because even though they can help you mitigate risks associated with scaling up your business, you might still be exposed to unknown risks that your partner might be struggling with. Therefore, don't just look at it from the perspective of what you stand to gain from the partnership, but also consider the flip side—the risks you might be inheriting from your partner.

When done properly, however, this strategic alliance can boost your growth prospects in terms of shared resources, cost mitigation, and shared responsibilities within your partner network. It gets even better if your partners share your values and objectives.

Advanced Tips

As you continue in the business, you'll need to explore some advanced strategies to position your business for successful scaling up, driving sustainable growth, and to realize your long-term strategic objectives.

Here are some brilliant ideas you should explore:

- **Invest in Technology and Automation**

Embrace technology solutions that streamline processes, improve efficiency, and enable scalability. Implementing advanced software systems for customer relationship management (CRM), enterprise resource planning (ERP), and automation of routine tasks can enhance productivity and free up resources for strategic initiatives.

- **Focus on Talent Acquisition and Development**

Invest in recruiting top talent and developing existing employees to build a high-performing team capable of driving growth. Offer competitive compensation packages, provide opportunities for professional development and training, and foster a culture that values innovation, collaboration, and continuous learning.

- **Diversify Revenue Streams**

Explore opportunities to diversify your revenue streams by offering complementary products or services, entering new markets, or expanding into adjacent industries. This can help reduce dependence on any single source of revenue and provide additional sources of income to support sustainable growth.

- **Optimize Supply Chain and Logistics**

Streamline your supply chain and logistics operations to improve efficiency, reduce costs, and enhance flexibility. Work closely with suppliers, distributors, and logistics partners to optimize inventory management, minimize lead times, and ensure seamless delivery of products or services to customers.

Chapter 8:

The Road to Recurring Income

Passive income and recurring income are two distinct financial concepts that play important roles in financial planning, especially when starting a business. Passive income refers to earnings from activities in which you are not actively involved. This type of income generally requires an initial investment of time or money but then generates returns without significant ongoing effort. Common examples include:

- rental income

- dividends from stocks or mutual funds

- royalties from intellectual property, like books or music

- interest income from savings accounts, bonds, or other investments

The key characteristic of passive income is its relatively hands-off nature once the initial setup or investment is complete.

Recurring income, on the other hand, refers to earnings that are received at regular intervals from consistent business activities. This type of income requires ongoing effort to maintain. Examples include:

- subscription services from customers for continuous access to products or services.

- monthly or annual fees from club or service members.

- continuous payments for ongoing services, such as maintenance or consulting.

Recurring income promises a predictable revenue stream, which is crucial for the stability and growth of your business. For your startup, the distinction between passive and recurring income is particularly important. Here are key reasons why you should focus on recurring income:

- Recurring income provides a steady and predictable cash flow, essential in managing operating expenses, reinvesting in the business, and ensuring long-term sustainability.

- Building a model based on recurring income encourages ongoing customer relationships and loyalty, which can lead to higher customer lifetime value and reduced churn rates.

- Businesses with a strong recurring income model are often valued higher than those reliant on one-time sales because they demonstrate stability and predictability to investors.

- A reliable recurring income stream allows for better planning and resource allocation, as revenue forecasts become more accurate and dependable.

- Offering subscription-based services or products can differentiate your business from competitors, providing a unique value proposition and consistent customer engagement.

As a small business owner, passive income takes a back seat because running a business typically involves active management and continuous effort. The nature of a small business means you must constantly engage in activities, for example, ensuring customers are satisfied and addressing their needs promptly, continuously promoting the business to attract new customers and retain existing ones, and overseeing daily operations to maintain quality and efficiency.

Thus, while passive income can supplement your earnings, it's the recurring income that forms the backbone of a successful and sustainable small business. Focusing on building and maintaining recurring income streams helps ensure that your business thrives in the long term, providing stability and growth opportunities that passive income alone might not offer.

Outsourcing

The fact that you can delegate some functions and focus on core activities to enhance your efficiency and reduce costs makes outsourcing an important consideration when planning for recurring income.

Outsourcing frees up valuable time to concentrate on the primary activities that generate income. For example, you could outsource administrative tasks, customer service, or IT support and instead, focus on refining your product or service range, and building stronger customer relationships.

External providers generally offer services at a lower cost due to economies of scale, specialized expertise, and advanced technology. Outsourcing gives you access to a pool of specialized skills and knowledge that might not be available in-house. Similarly, you could also outsource special functions like product development to ensure your product range remains innovative and appealing to your customers.

One thing you'll appreciate about outsourcing is the flexibility to scale your operations up or down according to your immediate needs, without the constraints of hiring and training new employees. This agility is particularly beneficial if you operate in an industry that experiences seasonal variations in customer traffic. Outsourcing makes it easier to plan for such situations, and maintain a predictable level of recurring income.

By outsourcing certain functions, you can mitigate risks associated with operational inefficiencies, compliance issues, and technological advancements. External providers are often well-versed in industry best practices and regulations, helping you avoid potential risks that could disrupt your projected income. In the long run, customer satisfaction is crucial for recurring income. Therefore, even as you explore options to outsource operations, never lose sight of your customers' needs. After all, you understand them better than your outsourcing partners.

Hiring the Right People

Whether you're starting the business or scaling up operations, working with the right people makes a big difference. The right people will help you realize your dream faster, because they're committed to the same goals that you are. As far as your journey to recurring income is concerned, staffing is one area you cannot take for granted.

Many businesses struggle with a high employee turnover, which eats into their profits. This is because each time you hire new people, you have to spend on recruitment, training, and other intangible costs like the cost in terms of the duration it takes them to get used to your business process.

With this in mind, you need to be proactive in your approach to hiring, and make sure that you bring in people who can buy into your vision. Employees with the necessary skills and experience will bring a transformative experience to your workforce in whichever roles they are tasked with. Here's an objective look at how to go about the hiring process:

- **Training and Development**

Investing in the training and development of your staff can help you set and maintain high standards in your business. Well-trained employees are more efficient, productive, and capable of delivering high-quality services, which will support your income-generation agenda.

- **Employee Retention**

Try to retain experienced and skilled employees to ensure consistency and reliability in service delivery. Long-term employees have a deeper understanding of your business processes and customer needs, leading to improved customer satisfaction and loyalty.

- Enhancing Customer Experience

Your staff directly influences the customer experience. Employees who are well-trained and motivated can provide excellent service, addressing customer issues promptly and effectively. Positive customer interactions build trust and loyalty, encouraging ongoing subscriptions or repeat business.

- Optimizing Operations

By strategically allocating staff based on their strengths and expertise, you can enhance productivity and service quality. This optimization ensures that all aspects of your business from product development, sales, and customer support, are running smoothly and effectively.

Ultimately, your approach to staffing plays a significant role in cost management, which directly affects your income. Think about the number of employees you need, their roles, and more importantly, whether you're bringing in people with the right attitude and personalities into your business. Go beyond their skills on paper and pay attention to the soft skills, because that's where you derive the most value from their contribution to your business.

Running a Simple, Efficient Operation

Simplicity is crucial for startups. As you navigate the early stages of your business, maintaining simplicity in various aspects will influence your success and sustainability. Starting with a simple value proposition makes it easier for potential customers to understand what you offer and why they need it. A clear, straightforward message helps you cut through the noise and quickly capture their attention. This clarity is essential for attracting and retaining customers, which is vital for your startup's growth.

How does this approach tie into your plan for recurring income?

When your products or services are simple and easy to understand, customers are more likely to see their value quickly. A clear and compelling offering makes it easier for customers to decide to subscribe or commit to a recurring payment model. Simplifying your offerings ensures that potential customers know exactly what they are getting, which helps build trust and encourages them to engage with your business on a recurring basis.

A simple and intuitive user experience is crucial for retaining customers in a recurring income model. When your subscription process is straightforward and your service is easy to use, customers are less likely to encounter frustrations that might lead them to cancel. Ensuring that every interaction is smooth and hassle-free keeps customers satisfied and loyal, directly contributing to recurring income.

In the long run, a simple operation means fewer moving parts and less complexity to manage. This efficiency allows you to focus on consistently delivering high-quality products or services, which is essential for maintaining recurring income. Streamlined operations mean fewer errors, quicker responses to issues, and a more reliable service, all of which enhance customer satisfaction and retention. By simplifying your business, you can concentrate on what you do best. Focus on your core strengths to deliver superior value to your customers, which is critical for maintaining recurring income.

Chapter 9:

Passion and Motivation

What drives you to work this hard? What keeps you on the grind, toiling to make sure this business is a success? When you look back, say five or ten years down the line, how would you wish to describe your entrepreneurial journey? These are the questions I need you to reflect on at the end of this chapter.

A strong sense of purpose makes a big difference in the trajectory of your business. We've talked about important steps throughout this book, for example, commitment to continuous learning and growth, seeking inspiration from successful peers, and celebrating small victories along the journey. Your success depends on these factors. From the moment you start as a sole-proprietor to the time you achieve your expansion goal and have a number of employees working for you, it will be an incredible journey, fueled by passion and motivation. You have to be passionate about your business, because that's the only way you'll convince your employees to buy into your vision.

Sure, being optimistic isn't always going to be a walk in the park. I mean, there will be difficult moments, some that you might even imagine impossible to get through. Yet, somehow, you'll find a way. In this chapter, we'll explore the dynamics of resilience in running a successful business, and draw inspiration from some of the biggest, most successful names in modern history.

Resilience is your secret weapon as an entrepreneur, keeping you passionate and motivated regardless of the challenges you face from time to time. While setbacks are a normal part of entrepreneurship, a resilient mindset helps you look at these obstacles not as roadblocks but as opportunities for growth and learning. With this mindset, you create a culture of enthusiasm and dedication to your goals and objectives. This drive rubs off on your team, inspiring confidence in your leadership. Resilience allows you to sustain your passion by focusing on long-term goals rather than being discouraged by short-term failures. This is how you learn to adapt to changes, innovate, and seek new paths when the original plan doesn't work out. A resilient entrepreneur is someone who stays committed to the vision and keeps pushing forward no matter what.

When things are not going your way, the last thing you want to do is cast a cloud of negativity in your workplace. This will not only dampen the spirits of your team, but can also have them doubting whether they're in the right place. Instead, maintain a positive outlook. This doesn't mean being delusional, but accepting the situation as it is, and encouraging your team that better things lie ahead. Maintain a proactive approach, try different solutions, and be optimistic about future possibilities. This positive energy will effectively create a supportive environment that enhances overall productivity and success across the board.

The way I see it, resilience is the cornerstone of sustained passion and motivation in your entrepreneurship journey. It will empower you to overcome adversity, stay focused on your goals, and continually pursue excellence, ensuring that you remain driven and inspired throughout your entrepreneurial journey.

Maintain the Passion, Against All Odds

In Chapter 6, we discussed common obstacles facing businesses, and highlighted some strategies you can implement to overcome them. The fact is that even the most resilient of us get overwhelmed sometimes, and that's just a part of life. There might even be moments when you question your decision to get into business in the first place. How do you stay positive through such tribulations? Sure, you're committed to your vision for the business, but being passionate can at times be easier said than done. If you have a seven-year plan for your business, you must have yearly milestones. The yearly milestones must also have quarterly check-ins, further broken down into monthly reviews, and weekly journals ... you get the drift, right?

When you do that, you're creating an elaborate blueprint for success. You don't just know where you want to be in seven years—you also know every step you must take to get there. This way, if something changes along the way, you can tweak your plan accordingly without losing the plot. For example, you've have a bad year, and sales were not so great. If you don't have an elaborate plan, this year could derail everything. On the other hand, if you had milestones and regular check-ins, you'd know what to tweak in your plans, or where to experiment with a new strategy and stay the course of your vision. Besides, such a plan answers the "why" for your vision, and that's where your passion comes from. You don't just know what you want to achieve in seven years, but also why it matters to you.

Progress doesn't happen overnight, so you must remind yourself regularly that every step, every obstacle, and every win brings you closer to your ultimate vision. Even when things are not going your way, you have to be passionate about your business for the following reasons:

- It's the drive that keeps you working towards your goals, the confidence and determination you need to power through the setbacks and inspire everyone else around you.

- If you're passionate about your business, you will always find a way to be resilient, and to stay focused and committed. How else do entrepreneurs manage to bounce back and keep moving forward?

- Think of all the innovators and creatives you know today. You can see how passionate they are about their craft. When you're passionate about something, thinking outside the box comes so easily for you because you're always willing to explore new ideas to make your ultimate goal better.

- Put yourself in your customers' shoes for a moment, and imagine what it feels like trying to engage a business owner who's not passionate about their work. The negative energy would rub you the wrong way, and you probably won't do business with them again. That's the thing about passion—

it's contagious. Customers can feel the enthusiasm, and easily build connections and loyalty with your brand. This is also how you build a community around your business.

- As a leader, your passion for your work inspires and motivates the people working with you. Over time, your team grows against the backdrop of a healthy working environment because you create the perfect recipe to attract not only talented members, but also partners and investors who are committed to your success because they can see, believe in, and share in your vision.

- There's a deep sense of personal fulfillment that comes with running a business you are passionate about. In this sense, we can think of passion as the link between your day-to-day activities in the business and the greater purpose you derive from your success.

Ultimately, passion is everything when running a business. When you go through difficult moments, lean on your support system. Surround yourself with people who are optimistic and generally have a positive outlook on life, whether they are entrepreneurs or not. Such people can help you see things from a different perspective, as well as advise and encourage you when all seems lost.

The fact that you are passionate about your business doesn't mean you are oblivious to the reality that unfolds before your eyes. As you draw inspiration from your support system, you must also be adaptable to change. The business world is dynamic, so things will never be the same. With the right mindset, you can learn how to pivot from time to time, be flexible, and adjust your business processes and strategies to better position your business without losing sight of your vision.

Passion and purpose go hand in hand. Never forget why you started this business in the first place, and the impact you hope to derive from it. While at it, be careful not to lose yourself in the pursuit of success to the extent that your business takes over your life. Sure, you love your work, but you must never forget to take care of yourself. Entrepreneurship can easily turn you into a workaholic, so much so that the boundaries between your work and personal life become nonexistent. Sleep well, get sufficient exercise, and reserve time for your hobbies. This is how you rejuvenate your spirit and keep the dream alive.

Be Inspired

Whether this is your first business or if you've been around for a while, it's always good to seek inspiration from people who have done some amazing work in their careers. You can learn a great deal from experienced and inspiring luminaries like Richard Branson, Oprah Winfrey, Steve Jobs, and Elon Musk, because you probably interact with a business, product or service they've influenced on a daily basis. Most of these people started from scratch, some even overcame extreme hardships to emerge victorious. As you learn about their success stories, find inspiration in their words. You'll find the following common themes in their stories:

- They share a deep passion for what they do and a clear sense of purpose, which proves that finding something you are passionate about can drive you through tough times.

- They faced setbacks from time to time but never gave up. Instead, those setbacks became launchpads for their success, and valuable learning points.

- They appreciate and value their customers. They realize that knowledge of customer needs is crucial in providing tangible, sustainable value.

- They are constantly looking for ways to disrupt the market and stay ahead of the competition. For long-term success in business, you must embrace an innovative mindset.

- They are always surrounded with talented and motivated individuals who understand, appreciate, and share their vision.

Building on this, let's now explore some inspirational quotes from some of the biggest names in the business world.

Oprah Winfrey

Oprah Winfrey, a media mogul and philanthropist, offers numerous pearls of wisdom that inspire entrepreneurs. One of her most powerful quotes is, "The biggest adventure you can take is to live the life of your dreams."

This quote reflects Oprah's journey from a challenging childhood to becoming one of the most influential women in the world. Throughout her career, she has taken bold steps to pursue her passions, from launching her own talk show and media network to advocating for education and social justice. Oprah's commitment to following her dreams and using her platform to make a positive impact has been the cornerstone of her success.

Oprah's quote and story highlight the importance of courage and authenticity. This sentiment encourages you to take risks and pursue your true passions, even when the path is uncertain or difficult. By daring to live the life of your dreams, you not only create a fulfilling and meaningful career for yourself but also have the potential to inspire and uplift others along the way. This mindset can help you navigate challenges and stay motivated during your entrepreneurial journey.

Melanie Perkins—Canva

Melanie Perkins, co-founder and CEO of Canva, has shared many insights over the years that are particularly inspiring for business owners. "If you can clearly articulate the dream or the goal, it's amazing what you can do."

This is a reflection of her approach to building Canva into a leading design platform. Perkins started with a clear vision: to democratize design and make it accessible to everyone, regardless of their skill level. Despite numerous challenges and rejections along the way, she never lost sight of her goal: to secure investment, build a strong team, and continually improve the product.

The lesson here is the power of having a clear and compelling vision. It highlights the importance of articulating your goals and dreams effectively, both to yourself and to others. When you communicate your vision clearly, you can inspire and mobilize people around you, attract the necessary resources, and navigate challenges more effectively. This clarity can turn your ambitious ideas into reality, just as Perkins did with Canva.

Elon Musk

Elon Musk might be a controversial figure from time to time, but his leadership in companies like X (formerly Twitter), Tesla, and SpaceX offer numerous insights that are profoundly inspirational for entrepreneurs. He once said: "When something is important enough, you do it even if the odds are not in your favor."

You can see Musk's unwavering commitment to his ambitious goals. Throughout his career, he has tackled incredibly challenging ventures, from electric cars and sustainable energy to space exploration and neural technology. Musk's determination and belief in the importance of his missions has driven him to persevere and achieve groundbreaking successes.

Musk's approach stresses the significance of passion and dedication. It serves as a reminder that when you believe deeply in the importance of your work, you must persist regardless of the difficulties and uncertainties. This mindset encourages you to pursue your vision with tenacity and resilience, knowing that great achievements often come from bold, determined efforts against the odds.

Confucius

Confucius, the ancient Chinese philosopher, provides timeless wisdom that continues to inspire entrepreneurs today. One of his most famous quotes is, "It does not matter how slowly you go as long as you do not stop."

The importance of perseverance and steady progress stands out in this quote. Confucius himself faced numerous challenges and setbacks in his life but remained dedicated to his studies and teachings. His commitment and persistence eventually led to profound influence on Chinese culture and beyond.

The words of Confucius serve as a powerful reminder that success is not always about speed but about consistency and endurance. His words encourage you to stay committed to your goals, regardless of how slow the progress may seem. By continually moving forward and not giving up you can overcome obstacles and achieve your aspirations over time.

Finally, never stop learning. Stay curious and constantly seek new knowledge. Embrace new trends and technologies, especially those that can transform your business processes. Your business might just be the beginning of something great, an enterprise that doesn't just outlive you, but transforms the lives of millions of people beyond your wildest imagination.

Chapter 10:

Look to The Future

When you think about the future of your business there's a lot to be excited about. I mean, we're currently living in a world where technology and innovation are at your fingertips, with tools and opportunities that were once the exclusive preserve of large entities, easily available to everyone. This level of innovation has been quite a game-changer, so much that you can only be limited by your imagination. The question, therefore, is what do you intend to do with the resources at your disposal, and how can you make them fit into your plans for the future of your business?I mean, we're currently living in a world where technology and innovation are at your fingertips, with tools and opportunities that were once the exclusive preserve of large entities, easily available to everyone. This level of innovation has been quite a game-changer, so much that you can only be limited by your imagination. The question, therefore, is what do you intend to do with the resources at your disposal, and how can you make them fit into your plans for the future of your business?

As we delve into the future prospects of your business, we'll try to address two important questions that will have a profound impact on your trajectory for the future:

- How can I grow my team?

- How do I handle challenges and setbacks along the way?

These questions play a significant role in the future of your business because the people around you usually influence your perspective on different fronts, and for that reason, they could shape your idea of the future of your business. Secondly, and we've mentioned this severally in this book, entrepreneurship is not an easy journey. It can be a rewarding one depending on how you approach it, but let no one falsely convince you that it's going to be a walk in the park. Expect setbacks from time to time. Setbacks are like mistakes in life—they can knock you down, but they should never keep you down. In an innovative world, challenges and setbacks should be valuable learning points as you work toward your vision for the business.

In this chapter, we'll take an exploratory glimpse at the future, and how you can start planning for it today so that you run a business that easily adapts to changing market dynamics and customer needs. For example, imagine the power of AI and automation at your disposal. You can streamline operations, manage inventory efficiently, personalize marketing, improve customer experiences around the clock, and even predict market trends. By automating some of the repetitive or mundane tasks, you free up resources and focus on strategic aspects of growing your business.take an exploratory glimpse at the future, and how you can start planning for it today, such that you run a business that easily adapts to changing market dynamics and customer needs. For example, imagine the power of AI and automation at your disposal. You can streamline operations, manage inventory efficiently, personalize marketing, improve customer experiences round the clock, and even predict market trends. By automating some of the repetitive or mundane tasks, you free up resources and focus on strategic aspects of growing your business.

Handling Challenges and Setbacks

Failure is a normal part of business. However, this doesn't mean you have to accept it as it is. If you conduct a quick search online about small businesses and failure, the statistics could dampen your spirit. the thing about failure is that you don't always have to wait to learn from your own. You can draw insight from someone else's failure, and take a different approach to your business so you don't end up in the same situation. For example, here's a list of common points of failure that many businesses experience: The thing about failure is that you don't always have to wait to learn from your own. You can draw insight from someone else's failure, and take a different approach to your business so you don't end up in the same situation. For example, here's a list of common points of failure that many businesses experience:

- Wrong approach to hiring—you cannot grow your business with the wrong people around you.

- Building a dead-end business—this is a business that, simply put, wasn't built on a foundation of growth. It's essentially crippled at birth.

- Loss of core team members—people come and go, so this is normal. However, the problem comes in when you do not have a system in place to replace such members, or one that uplifts individuals within your team to fill such positions. Looking outside for solutions that could be provided from within is demoralizing to your team.

- Losing major clients—this, unfortunately, is also a normal experience in business. You might even outgrow each other to the point where you no longer serve each other's needs.

- Building a business around a weak product or service.

- Insufficient cash flow, especially as a result of mismanagement and financial impropriety.

The problems above have scuppered the futures of many entrepreneurs, yet they have been widely documented. With a wealth of information at your disposal, you can certainly try to build a business that does not succumb to the same fate.

Failure, therefore, is an eventuality that you can avoid. What you cannot avoid, however, are setbacks and challenges. They are part of the journey, and how you cope with these obstacles can define your success. First, embrace resilience. Things won't always go as planned, so you need to bounce back quickly. Most setbacks are temporary, so instead of dwelling on what went wrong, focus on what you can learn from the situation and how you can improve. This is how you turn challenges into opportunities for growth.

Be adaptable. The entrepreneurial landscape is dynamic so you must be flexible to survive the setbacks. Pivot your business model, adjust your strategies, and try new approaches from time to time. Agility makes it easier for you to respond better to market changes, customer needs, and unforeseen obstacles.

Do you have a strong support network? Surround yourself with mentors, peers, and advisors who can offer guidance, support, and encouragement. Don't be afraid to ask for help when you're facing difficulties. Connect with people who have been through similar experiences to gain valuable insights. More importantly, your support network is always a reminder that you're not alone.

When you're going through a difficult time, it's easy to wallow in misery and lose sight of your goals. Get out of that mindset. If anything, you should never lose sight of why you started the business in the first place. Remind yourself of your long-term objectives and the passion that drives you. Focus and motivation will make a big difference, especially when things are tough.

A smart approach to addressing setbacks is to break the problems down into smaller, manageable steps. At first glance, most problems feel overwhelming, and you'll probably wonder how you can solve everything at once. Instead of that, break things down and address each step one at a time. Along the way, remember to celebrate the small victories and build on that momentum until you work your way through the entire mess.

In the long run, remember that failure is not the end, but a stepping stone to success. Take a moment and analyze what went wrong, why it happened, and use that knowledge to make better decisions in the future. Embracing failure as part of the learning process can help you become a more resilient and effective entrepreneur.

Try and maintain a positive attitude through it all. When facing adversity, focus on what you can control, celebrate your successes, and be optimistic about the future. A positive outlook will boost your morale and rub off on your team, inspiring them to keep pushing forward.

Finally, don't lose yourself in the process. Running a business can be demanding, especially when you consider the rising cost of living, and many other dynamics that are outside your control. Your mental and physical well-being are just as important as your pursuit of success. Practice self-care, get enough rest, eat healthily, and find time to relax and recharge. Make stress management techniques like mindfulness and exercise a part of your routine, because they can also help you maintain a positive mindset and a better approach to handling challenges.

Growing Your Team

The people working with you are the backbone of your business. They are directly involved in driving innovation, strategy execution, and growth. Always prioritize cultural fit when hiring and building your team. Your culture reflects your values, mission, and work style. Employees who can embrace your culture easily help you create a harmonious and productive work environment. They're more likely to collaborate effectively and stay motivated. Therefore, do not limit yourself to the traditional skills when hiring. After all, the goal is to build a cohesive team that works well together, and create a positive and dynamic work environment.

More often, you'll realize that employees who are a cultural fit will easily adjust to different roles. Elastic skills are another crucial factor to consider when building your team. Elastic skills refer to the ability to stretch and adapt to various tasks and challenges as they arise. Roles in startups tend to evolve, and responsibilities can change from time to time. For this reason, hire people who are adaptable and willing to learn. This flexibility makes it easier for your employees to navigate the dynamic nature of a startup environment. At the same time, encourage continuous learning and, where possible, provide opportunities for your team to learn new skills.

Growth should happen naturally, so allow your team to grow at their own pace, just as you would wish to grow your business at your own pace. Everyone has a unique learning curve and career trajectory.

Recognize and respect these differences by providing personalized development plans and opportunities for advancement. You'll realize that while Some team members may thrive by taking on more responsibilities, others will do well at a steadier, gradual pace. Offering mentorship, training programs, and regular feedback can help your employees reach their full potential.

Remember, you must create an inclusive and supportive environment for everyone to thrive, and through their success, your business will thrive. Encourage open communication where team members feel comfortable sharing ideas, feedback, and concerns. This openness can bring forth innovative solutions. Celebrate your wins together, and learn from failures together to reinforce a sense of unity and collective purpose. At the end of the day, you're not just filling open positions in your business, you're bringing together people with unique personalities, dreams, and ideas on life in general, and asking them to buy into your vision for the business. Their dedication will make your dream a reality.

The Future of Your Business

What does the future hold for your business? Well, the right answer to this is that the future is in your hands. Thus, the appropriate question in this case, would be what do you want for the future of your business?

We briefly outlined the prospects of AI and automation at the beginning of this chapter, and I am certain that at this point in time you've at least had some experience with different AI solutions. It's incredible what you can do with AI, and the the most interesting thing about it all is that we haven't even seen the best of AI yet. The systems and AI models we're interacting with in 2024 are at best foundational. The AI space evolves rapidly, and things can only get better in the future.

Now, let's talk about some important things that you've already interacted with, which will continue to play an important role in the future of your business: digital commerce, and ethics and sustainability.

- **Digital Commerce**

E-commerce and digital platforms have transformed the business landscape, and will continue to do so. It's always surprising how you enjoy one unique aspect of digital commerce today, then a year from now, it's no longer the new in-thing, but a prerequisite for businesses. At that point, people will be excited about something else. This shows you just how fast things change in the business world.

We've moved on from businesses being limited to geographic locations, to small businesses expanding to serve global audiences. Don't limit yourself. Don't set up a dead-end business. You have the whole world at your disposal, so push your business beyond borders and tap into new revenue streams and growth possibilities. Use social media and digital marketing tools to grow your brand presence and engage with customers in real-time. Most successful businesses today have built loyal communities around their brands.

- **Ethics and Sustainability**

Sustainability and ethical business practices are becoming increasingly important to consumers. People don't just want to buy from your business, they want to know what you stand for. What's your stand on things like environmental conservation, animal rights, affirmative action, and so on. Granted, some of these matters could be contentious, and your personal opinion could land you in problems with your customers, or even your employees.

As a rule of thumb, separate your personal views from your business, especially on social media. More importantly, you don't always have to give an opinion on everything. Sometimes it's better to be quiet than voice your opinion on certain matters, because even if you do that on your personal social media account, people will take it as the moral stand of your business, and any fallback from that could hurt your business.

Embracing ethical and sustainable business practices will not only endear you to conscientious consumers, but you can be proud that you're contributing positively to society, adding purpose to your entrepreneurial journey.

If there's something you can look forward to about the future of your business, it's got to be exposure to resources. Business owners have access to more resources and support systems today than ever before, and the prospects are even better for the future. You can network with other entrepreneurs, learn from webinars and online courses, and engage mentors in different capacities. With such resources there's no reason for you not to upskill, at a personal level and even for your team. This is how you stay ahead of the pack, keep up with trends in the industry, and build a resilient business.

Bonus Chapter:

30-Day Business Launch Checklist

Do you have an actual plan for the business? So far, we've delved into the dynamics of starting your business, covering everything you need to know from brainstorming the idea to exploring what the future might hold. Away from this broad perspective, let's now take a practical view on running the business, with an overview of what your first 30 days could look like. Remember, this is but a guideline, so you can tweak it according to the finite characteristics unique to your business.

Day 1-5: Lay the Foundation

- **Day 1: Work on Your Ideas**

Start by clearly defining your business idea. Outline what your business will offer and how it will meet a need or solve a problem for your target market. Conduct thorough market research to understand demand, identify your competitors, and recognize potential challenges. You can conduct surveys, interviews, and online research to gather data. At this point, your unique selling proposition (USP) should be clear, and you should make sure it sets you apart from competitors.

- **Day 2: Business Plan**

Create your business plan. A good business plan should feature your business model, target audience, revenue streams, and marketing strategy. Include sections on your business's mission, vision, and goals. Detail your financial projections, including startup costs, expected revenue, and break-even analysis. Reference the discussion we had in Chapter 2 to get you through this.

- Day 3: Business Registration and Legal Structure

Choose the legal structure that best fits your business (e.g., sole proprietorship, partnership, LLC, corporation). Each structure has different legal and tax implications. Register your business name with the appropriate authorities, ensuring it is unique and compliant with local regulations. Research and apply for the necessary licenses and permits based on your industry and location.

- Day 4: Financial Planning

Open a business bank account separate from personal accounts. The goal here is to simplify bookkeeping and tax filing. If you need to, create accounting systems using software like QuickBooks or Xero to track expenses, income, and manage invoices. Once this is done, create a financial plan that will guide your budget through your initial funding needs, ongoing expenses, and projected revenue. This plan will also help in cash flow management.

- Day 5: Building a Brand

What image do you want to project to customers? Create a logo that visually represents your brand and appeals to your target audience. Think of a color scheme and typography that represents your brand identity and values. As you work on the logo, images, and color, remember that the goal is to build a strong, consistent brand that your customers can recognize easily and trust.

Day 6-10: Branding and Your Online Presence

- Day 6: Domain & Website

Buy and register a domain name in your business name and make sure it is easy to remember. Choose a reliable website hosting service to ensure your site is fast and secure. Get someone to build you a basic website with essential pages such as Home, About, Services/Products,

Contact, and Blog. A good website should be mobile-friendly and optimized to rank well on search engines. First impressions are important, and since the website is your digital storefront, make sure the design is a value-add to your business.

- **Day 7: Get on Social Media**

Every credible business has an account on social media platforms like Facebook, Instagram, LinkedIn, and Twitter, so don't be left out. Use your brand style guide to maintain consistency in visuals and messaging. Add essential information on your profiles, for example, your bio, contact details, and links to your website. Create a content strategy where you regularly engage with your audience, post updates, and share content.

- **Day 8: Product/Service Development**

Finalize your product or service offerings. If you sell physical products, make sure you have sufficient inventory and packaging materials. For services, clearly define the packages or tiers if necessary. Create product documentation such as user guides and FAQs, and make them easily accessible on your website, social media page, and in the business premise.

- **Day 9: Pricing Strategy**

This is an important step because you don't want to price your business out of the market. At the same time, do not set your prices too low. If you do, you're either leaving money on the table, or people think your brand is substandard. Think about the cost of goods, competitor pricing, and perceived value. Your prices should cover the cost of doing business, and at the same time, allow you a reasonable profit margin. This is as much about your market positioning as it is about your desired profitability.

- **Day 10: Supply Chain Setup**

Identify reliable suppliers and negotiate favorable terms. Good relationships with suppliers who can meet your quality standards and delivery timelines are non-negotiable. To streamline your operations, make sure the order and delivery processes are efficient. For example, use inventory management systems, order tracking, and fulfillment logistics programs to help you ensure product availability and customer satisfaction.

Day 11-15: Marketing & Sales Strategy

- Day 11: Marketing Plan

What are your marketing objectives? For example, think about brand awareness, lead generation, or customer acquisition. Identify relevant marketing channels based on your target audience. Create a content calendar to show what, when, and where you will post content. An effective marketing strategy should include a mix of content types, for example, blog posts, videos, and social media updates, to engage your audience effectively.

- Day 12 -13: Sales Strategy

What are your sales targets and how do you intend to achieve them? Design a sales funnel that guides prospects from awareness to purchase. If you have a sales team, train them on how to engage potential customers and close deals. Use Customer Relationship Management (CRM) systems to track interactions, manage leads, and convert them into paying customers.

- Day 14-15: Advertising

Set up advertising accounts, for example Google Ads and Facebook Ads, and use them to create marketing campaigns targeting your ideal customer demographics. This also means allocating a budget for each campaign, with clear performance metrics to track progress and success. Monitor and optimize your ads to maximize ROI.

Day 16-21: Operational Setup

- **Day 16: Operational Plan**

This is about your daily operations, and processes that will keep the business running smoothly, and will include workflows for things like order processing, customer service, and inventory management. You can also create protocols for your customer service team on how to handle inquiries, complaints, and returns efficiently. The goal here is to ensure consistency, especially in the material used to train new employees.

- **Day 17: Technology & Tools**

What tools will be used in running your business? I'd encourage you to explore different options, read reviews, and if possible, try their demo accounts before purchasing premium or full packages. Do this for email marketing tools, project management tools, CRM tools, and any other tools relevant to your business. The trial experience will help you choose tools that save time, can integrate smoothly to streamline operations, and improve efficiency.

- **Day 18: Team Building**

This might not be necessary if you're running a sole-proprietorship, but as long as you're bringing one or more people on board, you must figure out the dynamics of their roles and functions, including compensation and benefits. More importantly, anyone who's joining the team should be aware of the business goals and culture.

- **Day 19: Pre-Launch Marketing**

Build anticipation for your launch with a countdown on social media and your website. You can also share behind-the-scenes content, teasers, and sneak peeks to get people excited. Send teasers to your followers and people on your mailing list, with exclusive pre-launch deals or early access.

- Day 20: Soft Launch

Test your systems and gather initial feedback with a soft launch. Invite a small group of friends, family, or loyal customers to use your product or service. Engage them and encourage honest feedback so you can address any issues that arise. From here, you can make necessary adjustments before the official launch, ensuring a smoother rollout.

- Day 21: Official Launch

Following the soft launch, announce the official launch across all platforms. If you have the budget for it, consider hosting a launch event or webinar to introduce your business and engage with your audience directly. Offer special promotions or discounts to attract more participants.

Day 22-25: Post-Launch Activities

- Day 22: Customer Relationship Management

Create a customer feedback loop to gather insights and improve your relationship with customers. Encourage them to leave reviews and feedback. Do your best to provide exceptional customer service by addressing inquiries and resolving issues promptly.

- Day 23: Continuous Marketing

Update your social media profiles with new and engaging content. Monitor your marketing campaigns and adjust strategies accordingly. Experiment with different types of content and marketing channels to find the most effective approach that will help you maintain momentum and attract new customers.

- Day 24: Financial Management

This will be useful once the business is up and running. Are you meeting your financial targets? Are you working within your budget or do you need to adjust the budget? Stay on top of bookkeeping and financial reporting to avoid nasty surprises, and run a sustainable business that's primed for growth.

- Day 25: Growth Strategies

You should constantly be on the lookout for opportunities to scale your business. For example, consider expanding your product line or entering new markets, strategic partnerships or collaborations that can help you reach a wider audience. Entrepreneurship is a journey of continuous innovation and adaptation to changing market conditions.

Day 26 and Beyond: Post-Launch Activities

- Day 26: Ongoing Customer Engagement

Keep engaging your customers online. Invite them to loyalty programs, special discounts, or exclusive content to keep them coming back. Constantly update your blog or social media platforms with valuable information to keep your audience engaged and informed.

- Day 27: Performance Analysis

Analyze your key performance indicators (KPIs) to gauge the health of your business. Explore metrics like the cost of customer acquisition and conversion rates. This data can help you refine your strategies and make smarter decisions that ultimately get you closer to achieving your business goals.

- **Day 28: Networking**

Sign up for local industry events, join business groups, and network with other entrepreneurs. A strong network can provide valuable insights, support, and opportunities for collaboration. This is an ongoing process, so it doesn't necessarily have to happen only on Day 28. Always be on the lookout for opportunities to reach out and engage with other entrepreneurs, and add them to your events calendar.

- **Day 29: Innovation**

Like networking above, you must continuously look for ways to innovate and improve your products, services, and processes. Learn about industry trends and emerging technologies. Encourage feedback and suggestions from your team and customers, and use this to reinvigorate and keep your business relevant and competitive.

- **Day 30: Long-Term Planning**

From the moment you get into the business world, think long term. Review your business plan and update it based on your experiences and feedback from the first month. Do this for each month, such that by the end of the year, you can identify trends or patterns you can use to readjust your business strategy going forward. Remember that in the long run, your business plan must align with your vision and the prevailing market conditions.

As we mentioned at the beginning of this chapter, use this checklist as a guide to get you through the first month of business. You can make adjustments according to your immediate needs, and the nature of your business, or the industry you operate in. It is a systematic and effective approach that easily walks you through essential matters that most first-time business owners struggle with.

Conclusion

Oh, what an amazing journey we've had so far! If there's one thing I hope you took from this book, it's that nothing's standing in your way. One of the biggest reasons why many people are afraid of starting a business is lack of finances. We explored this in-depth, showing you various options you can explore to set up a business, even if you don't have all the money you need. Never let finances stand in the way of your vision. The world of business is awash with opportunities that you can tap into and transform your life … and that's the core concept of this book, equipping you with the essential knowledge and tools to turn your business idea into a thriving reality.

Looking back, it's evident that starting a business is both an exciting and challenging experience. From brainstorming several ideas to executing your business plan, each step requires careful planning, dedication, and resilience. We walked through each of the important stages, sharing vital tips for beginners and advanced users alike. Your success will always come down to how well you understand your market, because without your customers, you have nothing.

Speaking of customers, always think about value addition. This is what all successful entrepreneurs swear by. Don't just start a business to offer a product or service—do something that adds value to the lives of your customers. If they wake up one day and your business is extinct, would this disrupt their lives, or would they just move on like nothing happened? A business that imprints on customers' lives will always have a loyal community built around it, and that's what you should aspire to achieve.

As you work on your business, remember that nothing is cast in stone. This particularly applies to your plans. Entrepreneurship is a dynamic ecosystem, one that demands adaptability from business owners. If events in the tech world are anything to go by, we live in a world that's constantly and rapidly evolving, so you have to stay flexible. Make a habit of reviewing your plans from time to time to ensure that the blueprint still works. Adaptability also means being ready to adjust and pivot your strategy in line with changing customer needs, demands, and preferences, and seizing new opportunities as soon as possible.

As we've mentioned severally throughout this book, build a customer-centric business. Their feedback will go a long way in ensuring your long-term success. Customer feedback should also inspire a spirit of continuous learning, because the more information you have, the easier it is to rethink your business strategy, marketing, and other elements crucial to your success. Be particularly keen on trend changes within the industry because these will always have a direct impact on your business.

Finally, manage your finances wisely. Know the difference between your personal money and the business' money. Pay attention to your cash flow, and invest in growth opportunities. As much as your business might be thriving, do not limit yourself. Consider diversifying into other ventures to spread your risks, especially if one sector of the economy is struggling. More importantly, always strive to maintain a healthy balance between expenses and revenue.

Challenges are inevitable in business. Embrace a growth mindset to stay resilient, learn from your setbacks, and persist in the face of adversity. This determination will be crucial in your success. With your comprehensive understanding of what it takes to set up and run a successful business, it's time to put your knowledge into action. Start by revisiting your business plan, setting clear goals, and outlining the immediate steps you need to take. Remember, every big success starts with a small step. Even if you are setting up as a sole proprietor, no one goes it alone. Engage others in the wider entrepreneurial community, seek advice from time to time, and never hesitate to iterate on your ideas. The business world is dynamic, but your ability to adapt and grow will set you apart from the competition.

Glossary

Accounting: The process of recording, summarizing, and reporting financial transactions to provide information useful in making business decisions.

Angel Investor: An individual who provides capital to startups in exchange for ownership equity or convertible debt.

Assets: Resources owned by a business that have economic value and can be used to meet debts, commitments, or legacies.

Balance Sheet: A financial statement that summarizes a company's assets, liabilities, and shareholders' equity at a specific point in time.

Bootstrapping: Starting and growing a business using personal finances or the company's own revenue without external funding.

Branding: The process of creating a unique image and identity for a product or business in the consumer's mind through marketing and promotional activities.

Business Plan: A formal written document outlining the goals, strategies, target market, and financial projections for a business.

Cash Flow: The total amount of money being transferred into and out of a business, especially as it affects liquidity.

Competitive Analysis: The process of evaluating the strengths and weaknesses of current and potential competitors to identify opportunities and threats.

Corporation: A legal entity that is separate and distinct from its owners, offering limited liability and the ability to raise capital through stock.

Demographics: Statistical data relating to the population and particular groups within it, used to identify target markets.

Due Diligence: The comprehensive appraisal of a business undertaken by a prospective buyer, especially to establish its assets and liabilities and evaluate its commercial potential.

Equity: The value of ownership interest in the business, calculated as the total assets minus total liabilities.

Exit Strategy: A planned approach to terminating a business operation or position in a financial investment, specifying the method of liquidation.

Financial Projections: Estimates of future revenue, expenses, and profitability, often included in a business plan to assess viability and attract investors.

Franchise: A type of license that a party (franchisee) acquires to allow them to have access to a business's (franchisor) proprietary knowledge, processes, and trademarks in order to sell a product or provide a service under the business's name.

Gross Profit: The difference between revenue and the cost of goods sold, representing the profit a company makes after deducting the costs associated with making and selling its products.

Intellectual Property (IP): Creations of the mind, such as inventions, literary and artistic works, designs, and symbols, names, and images used in commerce.

Inventory: The raw materials, work-in-progress products, and finished goods that are considered part of a business's assets and ready for sale.

Liabilities: A company's financial debts or obligations that arise during the course of its business operations.

Limited Liability Company (LLC): A business structure that offers personal liability protection and pass-through taxation to its owners.

Market Research: The process of gathering, analyzing, and interpreting information about a market, including information about the target audience and competitors.

Net Profit: The amount of money left after all expenses, taxes, and costs have been deducted from total revenue.

Operating Expenses: The expenses required for the day-to-day functioning of a business, excluding the cost of goods sold.

Partnership: A business arrangement in which two or more individuals share ownership and the responsibilities of running the business.

Revenue: The total income generated by the sale of goods or services related to the company's primary operations.

Scalability: The capability of a business to grow and manage increased demand without compromising performance or losing revenue potential.

Sole Proprietorship: A business owned and operated by a single individual, with no legal distinction between the owner and the business entity.

Stakeholder: Any individual or group that has an interest in the success and progression of a business, including employees, customers, suppliers, and investors.

SWOT Analysis: A strategic planning technique used to identify Strengths, Weaknesses, Opportunities, and Threats related to business competition or project planning.

Target Market: A specific group of consumers at which a company aims its products and services.

Trademark: A recognizable sign, design, or expression which identifies products or services of a particular source from those of others.

Venture Capital: Financing provided by investors to startups and small businesses with long-term growth potential in exchange for equity or ownership stake.

Working Capital: The difference between a company's current assets and current liabilities, representing the short-term liquidity available for day-to-day operations.

References

Tackling small business burnout (2024). Ahead for Business. https://aheadforbusiness.org.au/resources/tackling-small-business-burnout#:~:text=Signs%20and%20symptoms&text=Feelings%20of%20energy%20depletion%20or

Ali, R. (2023, December 22). *4 steps to creating a financial plan for your small Business.* NetSuite. https://www.netsuite.com/portal/resource/articles/financial-management/small-business-financial-plan.shtml

Blakely-Gray, R. (2022, November 3). *Money management tips to keep your small business in shape.* Patriot Software. https://www.patriotsoftware.com/blog/accounting/small-business-money-management-tips/

Cantero-Gomez, P. (2022, October 12). *Basic structure of a business plan for beginners.* Forbes. https://www.forbes.com/sites/palomacanterogomez/2019/07/24/basic-structure-of-a-business-plan-for-beginners/?sh=3d4992bd2ad3

Carter, R. (2021, April 27). *Could "entrepreneurial outsourcing" be your perfect lazy way to make a great second income.* Medium. https://roycarter-89394.medium.com/could-entrepreneurial-outsourcing-be-your-perfect-lazy-way-to-make-a-great-second-income-from-15847cfd9453

Cote, C. (2022, March 17). *How to do market research for a startup.* HBS Online. https://online.hbs.edu/blog/post/how-to-do-market-research-for-a-startup

Curtis, G. (2024, April 25). *Simple ways to keep your business going in hard times.* Investopedia. https://www.investopedia.com/articles/pf/09/keep-small-business-afloat.asp

DeMarco, J., & Anthony, L. (2021, June 4). *Startup funding: What it is and how to get capital for a business.* NerdWallet. https://www.nerdwallet.com/article/small-business/startup-funding

Expanding product or service offerings (2024). Faster Capital. https://fastercapital.com/startup-topic/Expanding-Product-or-Service-Offerings.html#:~:text=Expanding%20product%20or%20service%20offerings%20is%20a%20crucial%20strategy%20for

Freedman, M. (2018, May 21). *10 Tips for managing small business finances.* Business News Daily. https://www.businessnewsdaily.com/5954-smb-finance-management-tips.html

Haan, K. (2024, April 7). *How to start a business in 11 steps.* (2024 Guide). Forbes. https://www.forbes.com/advisor/business/how-to-start-a-business/

Hoffower, H. (2019, February 10). *How to build long-term wealth through passive income and outsourcing.* Business Insider. https://www.businessinsider.com/financial-freedom-book-passive-income-outsourcing-build-wealth-2019-2?r=US&IR=T

How to overcome small business setbacks. (2022, September 15). Palmetto Payroll Solutions. https://palmettopayroll.net/how-to-overcome-small-business-setbacks/

How to scale your small business into something much bigger. (2024, February 13). Small Business Coach. https://www.smallbusinesscoach.org/how-to-scale-your-small-business-into-something-much-bigger/#:~:text=Setting%20Clear%20Goals%20and%20Objectives&text=Define%20your%20vision%20for%20growth

Jhajharia, S. (2023, April 19). *The benefits of strategic partnerships for scaling your business.* Growth Idea. https://growthidea.co.uk/blog/the-benefits-of-strategic-partnerships-for-scaling-your-business

Kopp, C. M. (2022, October 2). *What is brand awareness?* Investopedia. https://www.investopedia.com/terms/b/brandawareness.asp

Live And Learn Consultancy. (2013, March 22). *5 basic Sales tips for beginners.* https://www.liveandlearnconsultancy.co.uk/top-10-best-sales-tips-for-success/

Madden, T. (2024, February 2). *The small business owner's guide to resilience.* INC. https://www.inc.com/inc-masters/the-small-business-owners-guide-to-reillience.html#:~:text=Building%20resilience%20takes%20ongoing%20work

Miller, D. (2024, May 28). *5 innovative ways to run a more efficient small business.* SCORE. https://www.score.org/resource/blog-post/5-innovative-ways-run-a-more-efficient-small-business

Morrison, S. (2019, January 28). *11 things to do before starting a business.* Business News Daily. https://www.businessnewsdaily.com/1484-starting-a-business.html

Patel, B. (2024, March 27). *7 smart small business tax planning strategies to help you save money.* On Deck. https://www.ondeck.com/resources/high-value-tax-strategies-for-small-business-owners

Porteous, C. (2020, March 18). *A beginner's guide to small-business structures.* Entrepreneur. https://www.entrepreneur.com/starting-a-business/a-beginners-guide-to-small-business-structures/347246

Qualtrics. (n.d.). *How to increase brand awareness: 10 top strategies.* Qualtrics. https://www.qualtrics.com/experience-management/brand/how-to-increase-brand-awareness/

Rainey, J. (2023, August 25). *Navigating burnout as a small business owner: Tips for getting back on Ttack.* Jenna Rainey. https://jennarainey.com/navigating-burnout-as-a-small-business-owner-tips-for-getting-back-on-track/

Savva, S. (2024, March 25). *14 tips to manage stress as a small business owner.* Wave Apps. https://www.waveapps.com/blog/managing-stress-as-a-business-owner

Singh, S. (2024, February 19). Council post: Unlocking the secrets of successful entrepreneurs: Passion versus prudence. *Forbes.* https://www.forbes.com/sites/forbesbusinesscouncil/2024/02/13/unlocking-the-secrets-of-successful-entrepreneurs-passion-versus-prudence/?sh=1f45a2487c65

Strategies for effective debt management in small businesses. (2024, February 1). Xeinadin. https://xeinadin.com/blog/strategies-for-effective-debt-management-in-small-businesses/

TechnoServe. (2021, October 28). *Five reasons to be excited for the future of small business.* Techno Serve. https://www.technoserve.org/blog/five-reasons-to-be-excited-for-the-future-of-small-business/

The future of small businesses: What you need to know. (2022, March 24). Ring Central Blog. https://www.ringcentral.com/us/en/blog/future-of-small-businesses/

10 legal requirements for starting a small business. (2023, May 5). MBO Partners. https://www.mbopartners.com/blog/how-start-small-business/legal-requirements-for-starting-a-small-business/

Made in United States
North Haven, CT
29 March 2025